LESSONS

from the TRAIL

To Eric Metaxas:

Thank you for the work
that you do in service of our
Lord Jesus Christ.

Ike Andru

Spokane, WA

3/3/21

LESSONS
from the TRAIL

*Exploring the Intersection between
Grief and Adventure*

IKE ANDREWS

Trilogy Christian Publishers

A Wholly Owned Subsidiary of Trinity Broadcasting Network

2442 Michelle Drive

Tustin, CA 92780

For information, address Trilogy Christian Publishing

Rights Department, 2442 Michelle Drive, Tustin, Ca 92780.

Trilogy Christian Publishing/ TBN and colophon are trademarks of Trinity Broadcasting Network.

For information about special discounts for bulk purchases, please contact Trilogy Christian Publishing.

Manufactured in the United States of America

10 9 8 7 6 5 4 3 2 1

Library of Congress Cataloging-in-Publication Data is available.

ISBN 978-1-64773-586-9

ISBN 978-1-64773-587-6 (ebook)

ACKNOWLEDGMENTS

There is a facet of Jewish wisdom that recognizes one of the sacrifices God desires from man is anonymity. This is based on Micah 6:8, which says, "He has shown you, O mortal, what is good. And what does the Lord require of you? To act justly and to love mercy and *to walk humbly with your God.*" (NIV, emphasis added) I take this to mean that man should not seek to glorify himself but to recognize his deferential status before the Almighty.

So I approached this work not to extol anything that the man Brian Matthew Johnson did but to be candid and personal about his life as experienced through the eyes of a first-person chronicler who happened to also be a close friend. I hope to show that one does not need to be famous or powerful to have a significant impact on the lives of others. There are probably thousands and thousands of people living ordinary lives whose stories go untold and whose memories fade with each successive generation, but who have left the world a better place on account of what they did in between every breath of life that God blessed them with. This is the story of one of them, and you will discover vignettes of others like him in the following pages.

Thus, it is in this spirit of revelation that I attempt to stay true to the authoritative counsel in Micah 6:8. Just as importantly, I wanted to share insights along the way to the lessons that God taught me through my adventures with Brian and a few other individuals. To that end I am grateful to Dena Johnson and her brothers and sisters in Christ at the First Church of the Nazarene in Lewiston, Idaho, for allowing me to share their parts in this story. Same for the many friends with whom I've shared unforgettable escapades over the years and who are also mentioned in this book. In the few instances where I did not get permission to use peoples' names in these true events, I have changed those names to respect their privacy and innocence.

I also wish to thank Melody Paasch, founder of the on-line school Now Interpret This (www.nowinterpretthis.org), for allowing me to reproduce a Facebook post she made in August of 2014, as well as

Kelly Cach, who also permitted me to reproduce a Facebook post she made in that same timeframe. To my daughter Emily Andrews I extend my appreciation for sharing her artistic and technological skills in helping with the manuscript preparation. Lastly, I owe my son Zachary Andrews a huge debt of gratitude for all the hard work he did poring over an earlier draft of the manuscript and offering detailed editorial suggestions, as well as with helping with the chapter titles. His help was invaluable.

To God be all the glory…

TABLE OF CONTENTS

PROLOGUE

I stepped into the darkness of the house from the garage door entrance and reached for the light. A brilliant flash across the nighttime sky illuminated the room before I could flick the switch. I moved across the kitchen and through the sliding glass doors that led to our deck where I could see the edge of a severe storm moving into Spokane from the south. I stood there in awe, amazed at the serpentine streaks of fire that illuminated the clouds, turning them into gigantic Chinese lanterns. The energetic wind that bent the tops of the pine trees in our neighborhood carried along the loud rumbles of thunder that pealed through the valley. I backed away until I was in the kitchen again and encouraged Debbie to come and take a look at the mighty power of God's creation on display. We stood and stared in fearful reverence for a moment, unaware that we were witnessing a harbinger of a much greater storm to come.

We retired for the night, then hours later the first call came in. I slept soundly through it, but the ringing woke up Debbie. It was the house phone, the one we rarely answer since most of the calls we receive on it are spam. Besides, all of our family and friends have our mobile numbers. She let it go and tried to go back to sleep, but then she heard a second series of rings. A little worried that maybe our daughter on the east coast was trying to get a hold of us, she pulled herself out of bed, but the answering machine kicked in before she could pick up the phone. She then realized something didn't make sense—our daughter always used her mom's mobile number when she wanted to talk. Curious, Debbie started scrolling through the call history to find out who'd been trying to reach us so late at night. Just then she heard my cell phone vibrate. She answered it then hurried back into the bedroom and started vigorously poking her fingers into my shoulder blade. That's when I woke up.

"Something's happened to Brian," she said. "They want you at the hospital now."

Brian Johnson was my best friend and the most trusted brother in Christ that I had ever known, so hearing those words quickly dispelled the grogginess I felt from being pulled out of such a deep slumber. I swung out of bed, pulled the earplugs from my ears, and went to the closet to put on a pair of jeans. Then I grabbed my favorite T-shirt, one that had a screen print of a red, white, and green crankset. I had purchased it two years earlier at a bike store in Winthrop, WA, when Brian and I and two other friends spent a weekend mountain biking the trails in the Methow Valley. It seemed fitting that if I was going to tend to a crisis involving Brian, I should wear a memento from one of our mountain-biking adventures. After all, mountain biking was the sport that had brought us together and the catalyst that cemented the bonds of brotherhood and friendship that developed so deeply over the years we'd known each other.

"I'm coming with you to the hospital," Debbie said as she started getting dressed.

"All right," I acknowledged, heartened to have her accompany me.

I retrieved my phone and saw that I had two voicemails, one from Brian and one from an unknown caller. I listened to Brian's message first, unsure of what to expect but hoping that I would indeed hear Brian's voice, signaling that the crisis perhaps wasn't as bad as I feared. It turned out to be a message from Dan LejaMeyer, a school administrator who was also a friend of Brian's and a member of Brian's church, telling me to call him as soon as possible. I had gotten to know Dan a little bit from the few times he joined Brian and me on some trail rides. Dan had used Brian's phone to access the contact information for my mobile phone after the unsuccessful attempts to reach me on the house phone. His second attempt to reach me was when Debbie had answered, leading her to wake me up.

The unknown caller was Keesha Johnson, the wife of another friend of Brian's, a man named Todd Johnson (no relation to Brian). I knew them both on account of our daughters being on the high school track and cross-country teams together. Like Dan's voicemail, Keesha directed me with grim urgency to call as soon as possible, but added the instruction to get to Sacred Heart, a major hospital complex situated just south of the freeway in downtown Spokane, over a hundred miles from where Brian and his family lived in Lewiston, Idaho.

What's going on? I wondered. *Why are they coming to Spokane and not the hospital in Lewiston?* Oftentimes serious medical emergencies were referred to the Spokane hospitals, and it began to sink in that something really bad had happened. Just then a petrifying text from Brian appeared on my phone, which at that point I assumed Dan was sending: "Sacred Heart....Thanks for going. Very critical... On a ventilator....Head trauma."

"On my way," I hammered back, cognizant of the bleakness of his words and the paralyzing effect they seemed to have on my soul at the moment.

"Thanks. I'm texting from Brian's phone. Pray brother."

Just then Debbie emerged from the bedroom so I took Dan's command to task. Grabbing her hand, I said, "Let's pray." We embraced each other and opened our hearts to God, confessing our lack of knowledge about what had happened, acknowledging that we knew it was serious and that Brian, his wife Dena, and their three girls needed God's help at this moment. We prayed that God would see us through whatever we were about to encounter. If there ever was a time we needed to focus on our Lord, it was now.

FOCUS

We flew down the road, the magnificent Sawtooth Mountains living up to their name, towering in jagged relief against the eastern horizon. It was late afternoon, around seven, and the skies were still sunny and blue. We drove with the windows down and tunes blaring, our bikes secured on the vibrating rack hitched to the rear of the Xterra. Awash with joy and exhilaration, we gulped down deep breaths of high-altitude air, fueling our lungs with the oxygen we needed to sustain the flame of our passion for the weekend ahead and for life itself. A quick glance at the speedometer on one of the straight stretches showed seventy-five, a daring speed unfettered with worry of radar or merging traffic and recklessly blind to the dangers from wandering wildlife. My first generation iPod was hooked up to the radio via an AM transmitter adapter, and the best playlist I could assemble enhanced the enjoyment of the moment, the sound volume amped loud enough to blend with the rushing whir of the passing air. We talked as fast and free as we moved, unhampered by convention, like school boys just released into the first day of an infinite summer.

"I still can't believe we're doing this," Brian shouted above the din. "This is going to be a perfect weekend!"

"It doesn't get much better than this," I answered back, referring to both the surrounding scenery as well as the opportunity for some best-of-class mountain biking.

I felt blessed to have Brian Johnson as my partner for the weekend adventure that awaited us on the trails around Ketchum, Idaho. Even though he had mountain biked for only about five years, Brian had a natural affinity for riding on two wheels, probably honed from time spent on dirt bikes growing up in Western Washington. We'd been hitting the trails together since 2000, when a web developer on my staff at work learned about our common interest in the sport and brokered an introduction. Those early rides together were the foundation for building a deep and abiding friendship that would continue to develop over the years ahead, when I would come to appreciate him as the best mountain-biking companion a rider like me could ever hope to have.

Yet, for all the times we'd ridden together during the past four years, neither one of us had ever made a weekend trip devoted solely to our favorite pastime. The catalyst for changing that occurred in November 2003 at a magazine stand in the Little Rock Airport, where I purchased a bike magazine that had an article detailing the top five mountain-biking trails in the US. The magazine's editorial staff included the Imperial Gulch Trail in Ketchum in the list, and I became excited that such a prestigious trail was so close to home. I read the article several times on the plane ride home, then showed it to Brian the next day when I got back to the office. I re-read the trail description over his shoulder as he read it for the first time. It seemed to transport us into a wondrous trance as we envisioned a long, sweet singletrack traversing a high ridge of emerald green, then sly and fast descents, first into thick groves of conifers, then scraggly clusters of scrub brush, with majestic mountains ensconcing you like a pebble at the bottom of a well.

"Wow," Brian said when he had finished reading the article. "That sounds awesome."

"We've got to do it," I said emphatically. "We need to set a date and go for it."

Well, we didn't set a date that day, but throughout the dead of winter when we could only dream about mountain biking we started making plans for our first ever weekend trail riding adventure, far away from the usual weekend routines that occupy the attentions of hard-working, church-going family men. By spring we had settled on the date and cleared it with our wives. And now here we were, blazing through the Idaho countryside on to what we thought would be the best mountain-biking adventure ever.

We crossed Galena Summit and descended down the mountain toward Ketchum, watching the sun drop beneath the peaks of the pine trees just west of us. The road unraveled for about another ten miles until we reached the campsite we'd researched ahead of time to be the best place to set up our base. We turned in and drove around, looking at the available sites.

"How's this spot?" I asked, pulling into a level space next to a stream known as the Big Wood River.

"Looks good to me," Brian said.

I started unloading the camping supplies while Brian hurried over to the pay station.

"Wow, this is cheap!" he shouted at me. "Seven bucks per night."

He paid the fee for two nights and then we pitched the tent. When we were finished, I looked around and said, "You know, it looks like we're the only ones in the campground tonight."

Brian glanced around and nodded in agreement as a reverent hush descended over us, allowing us to fully experience the sublime solitude.

It didn't take long for our growling stomachs to interrupt the stillness, signaling that it was time to eat. Brian lit up the camp stove and boiled some hot water for the instant gourmet meals-in-a-pouch. It was going on nine thirty, and there was still enough ambient light in the sky to eliminate the need to fire up the lantern. Behind the mountain face to the west of us, the pale, outer corona of the sun continued to dim as it traced its way northwardly across the horizon. By ten thirty the faint glow gave way to the stars, which blazed forth like an atomic explosion of white-hot pinpricks against a black velvet canvas.

We slept and rose the next day without an alarm clock, crawling out of the tent into a frigid dawn. A trace of snow lay on the ground, and a bracing chill lingered about the campground, awaiting the ascendency of the sun with its warming rays to chase the cold away. We ate breakfast and then took off, first driving through Ketchum and then further south until we reached the turnoff to the Imperial Gulch trailhead, and then about three miles after that. Traveling there took longer than I thought, or maybe it just seemed that way on account of the anticipation building up for the ride.

Finally, we reached the trailhead parking lot, only the second car there at this early, chilly hour. We quickly unloaded our bikes and began the methodical putting-on of our gear—cleats, CamelBak hydration packs, sunglasses, helmets, and gloves, in that order. About ten minutes later we were ready, so we straddled our bikes and, under an emerging sun, we prayed for the upcoming ride before heading out.

Our plan was to take the Greenhorn Trail going up the mountain, a parallel route to the summit, then descend down Imperial Gulch where the two trails intersected. We'd also noticed from the map that a section of the Greenhorn Trail diverged within the first half mile or so, then reconnected shortly after that, forming a small loop. We thought we would take the loop's northern path, as it looked like it provided more interesting terrain to ride on. A little ways into the trail we came upon a small hill that got steeper toward the top, testing us immediately on how well we could engage the power stroke in our leg muscles to overcome this somewhat formidable hump. I hadn't warmed up enough to attack the climb, which is how some hills are best overcome, so I had to get off and push, but the adrenalin from the excitement of the unfolding ride motivated me to run the rest of the way up the hill.

We made a quick descent down to a tiny gulch and then back over another hump before landing at a three-way juncture. We took the trail to the right and the climb became more gradual. I noticed the sunshine had disappeared and it was getting chillier, even though I was sweating. So far we'd seen none of the epic scenery so glossily displayed in the bike magazine pages, just lots of low-lying brush, which gave way to scraggly trees as we furthered our way up the trail. The tree density started to thicken about an hour into the climb, right after a fairly wide stream crossing. The icy splash on my calves and into my shoes reminded me that there was still a snow-pack slowly melting and draining from the higher elevations.

Everything seemed to be rolling according to plan until we came to a fork in the trail. It wasn't obvious which way we should go and we both had different opinions about which path to take. I asked Brian to reach into my CamelBak and pull out the map so we could review our route again. It wasn't immediately apparent that we had made a wrong turn at the three-way juncture, which created a brief episode of consternation until we realized our mistake. Fortunately, the trail system networked in such a way that either path would ultimately circle back to the Greenhorn Trail, which would then connect us to the start of the Imperial Gulch descent. We would have to ride farther than we'd originally planned, but that didn't seem like such a big deal. After all, riding was what we were here to do.

We settled on taking the fork on the right, as that seemed like a better route, so we took off again. We pedaled on for about twenty minutes until I heard a sound like a giant branch snapping off a tree. Brian immediately hollered at me to stop. Turning around I saw him off his bike and bent over the real wheel hub. Seconds later I saw that his derailleur had broken. The thick metal part that's shaped like an elbow had split into two fragments, which now dangled from the loose and sagging chain.

"Wow! I've never seen this before!" I exclaimed.

"Neither have I," Brian responded with a tinge of frustration in his voice.

"What do you think we should do?" I asked.

Brian fiddled with the dangling metal pieces, trying to remove them from the sagging chain. "I don't know," he answered with bewilderment.

"I have a chain break tool," I offered optimistically. I reached into the back of my CamelBak and dug it out. It was the first time I'd ever packed one, and I silently thanked God for giving me the wisdom to add this to my repair kit. "Why don't we break the chain and shorten it to where you can at least use one gear. You'll only have that one gear, so you'll have to pick one that you think will be the most useful."

"Yeah, I think that would work," Brian answered, looking at the small, funny-shaped instrument that was still in its original blister packaging. "How does it work?"

"I don't know. I've never used one before," I admitted sheepishly.

"That makes two of us," Brian countered with a spark of humor.

We set about trying to fix the chain as gentle raindrops started pitter-pattering the surrounding terrain. It was a pleasant and relaxing sound that seemed to soothe the tension I felt in attempting to make the on-the-fly repair on Brian's bike. To compensate for the lack of facility in using the tool, we had to jointly manipulate it, which I think set a Guinness record for the total number of fingers that could simultaneously touch such a small implement. By the time we had figured out how to get the pin out of the linkage so we could break the chain, the rain sounds had picked up, the steadily-falling beads of water making a sound like a gentle drum roll. *At least we aren't getting very wet*, I thought to myself, since the canopy was thick enough to stop most of the precipitation from striking us.

After Brian put some thought on just what his single gear should be, we removed the second pin to shorten the chain to the corresponding length, but then we struggled to pin together the two ends so we could close the chain. To compound the difficulty, we were greeted with a one-two punch of lighting and thunder that heralded the arrival of a barrage of pelting hailstones. The icy pebbles penetrating through the tree limbs struck the shell of our helmets and bounced off with a unique popping sound, momentarily distracting our fumbling efforts to pin the chain back together. Finally, we managed to force the teeny rod through all the holes and complete the linkage as the hailstones relentlessly pummeled the landscape around us.

Relieved, I shouted, "Let's go," eager to start moving again to combat the icy chill that was settling in. I was poised to hop onto my bike and race back down the mountain when I turned to see if Brian was ready. He was, but not for going down the mountain. He was ready to resume the climb up to the summit, and his bike was pointed in that direction.

"What are you doing?" I asked incredulously.

"C'mon. We got to finish the ride," he replied calmly, as if there were no other alternative.

"We need to get off the mountain and out of this weather and get back into town and find a bike shop to fix your bike. You ought to be able to get a pretty good crank going downhill with that one gear you've got."

"No. We've come this far, we need to keep going. I can pedal up the mountain."

"What do you mean? You can't expect to crank up the mountain with just that gear. It's too high!"

"Yes I can. I don't mind pushing if I have to."

"Yeah, but because we took the wrong turn, there's going to be *lots* of pushing, based on those elevation lines on the map for this trail."

"I can push," Brian insisted. Suddenly there was a terrifying flash just above our heads, instantly followed by a concussive blast of thunder so loud and forceful that it shook the ground we stood on. "All right, let's go back," Brian abruptly conceded.

So we took off back down the way we came, rolling precariously over the hailstones that blanketed the trail like icy-white ball bearings, then across the stream where it no longer mattered how much water splashed on me, since I was now soaking wet all over. Brian had to bail out in the middle of the rushing water and push the rest of the way across since he couldn't get the power he needed to pedal through with the one gear he'd chosen. Soon we were on a rapid descent and losing elevation quickly. The hail had ceased falling and now only rain riveted from the sky.

Mud was flying out from under our wheels like miniature volcanic eruptions, much of it hitting my face and torso. My yellow-lensed eyewear had a sheen of water that made visibility difficult, and the couple of splotches of mud didn't help, either. I stopped so I could wipe my glasses clear and Brian whizzed on by. Mud was flinging out from under his rear tire, and some of the smaller granules landed in my mouth, tasting like wine dregs from a bold, unfiltered cabernet.

I resumed pedaling and was gaining on Brian as we approached the three-way juncture. "Take the lower section," I yelled, just so he wouldn't have to get off and push over the two hills. There was no way he could have heard me over the drumming of the rain, yet he figured it out anyway. We were really moving now, pumping furiously to pick up additional speed, propelled not by the usual desire just to go fast but by the overwhelming urge to get back to the Xterra where we could take shelter from the relentless deluge spilling out of the sky.

Next came a dip in the trail, followed immediately by a sharp turn, and Brian disappeared from my field of vision. I leaned right and low so I could take the turn as fast as possible and there, without warning, was a ravine fifteen to twenty feet deep, cut by the stream that up to this point had pretty much been a trailside feature. All that was left of the bridge crossing the ravine were four twelve-inch wide beams of timber, each about two feet apart. Since I had been so tight on the turn I was on track for taking the outermost beam on the right. Its surface was wet and slick and I was looking more at the bottom of the ravine than at the narrow plane of sodden wood. The next thing I knew my front wheel was riding the edge of the beam, and I could see the outermost knobs on the tire protruding over the abyss. There was only one thing to do: avert my eyes and look at the center of the beam.

The wheel stopped its starboard drift and I stayed on the edge of the beam, feeling the downward pull of gravity coupled with an incredible, rushing awareness of life and death hanging at the intersection of the horizontal and vertical planes of the timber. Time seemed to stop, as if I could never reach the other side, but at last my front wheel rolled off the wood and back onto the muddied trail, and I knew I was going to be all right. I hurried down the trail and caught sight of Brian again, and was relieved to see he had made it across the ravine okay. At that point I let out one of the loudest whoops I have ever cried out, loud enough to beat down the overwhelming fear that was rising inside of me as I realized just how close I came to having a painfully crippling or even fatal accident; so loud it seemed to echo throughout the canyons and valleys surrounding Imperial Gulch.

Somewhere long ago I had read in one of those "how-to-mountain bike" manuals that *where you look is where you go*. Mountain bikers call this their line...eyeing out along the ground in front of you where you want your forward trajectory to go, and that's where your wheels will end up making contact. That piece of advice had stuck with me and thank God I remembered it at a critical moment on the tail end of the Imperial Gulch trail. I am convinced it is what kept me from slipping over the edge and plunging into the ravine that rainy morning.

Matthew 14: 22-31 tells us that after Jesus fed the 5,000, he told His disciples to get in a boat and cross the Sea of Galilee without him. Sometime between three and six the next morning, the wind picked up and the disciples strained to keep the boat aright. Then they saw Jesus walking on the sea toward them, and they became even more troubled, thinking a ghost was visiting them. "But immediately Jesus spoke to them and said, 'Take heart. It is I. Do not be afraid.'" (v. 27, NRSV).

At that point, Peter asked Jesus to let him come to him on the water. Jesus beckoned him on, and Peter – much to his amazement, I'm sure – climbed out of the boat and began walking toward him. *But then he took his eyes off the line*, so to speak. He looked at the boisterous wind and waves and became afraid, and started sinking. He took his eyes off Jesus and started sinking.

This is the lesson I learned that day: Focus on what gives life. On a practical level, if you're mountain biking on a narrow beam across a deep ravine, keep your eye on the centerline of the wood. On the bigger ride through life, though, keep your eye on Jesus. Terrible news—personal tragedies, acts of terrorism, epidemics, riots, natural disasters, ethnic killings, persecution—all that stuff can easily divert your journey into a pit of despair and spiritual death. Following Jesus's line will bring you hope and inner peace and keep you from slipping over the edge. Keep your eyes on him.

THE ACCIDENT

Debbie and I made the trip to Sacred Heart Hospital in what seemed like record time, aided by deserted streets and traffic signals that only flashed yellow caution lights during the late hours of night. We pulled into the parking lot next to the ambulance entry area at around two thirty and worked our way through the labyrinth-like corridors to the emergency room ICU. The ambulance carrying Brian had already arrived, and so had Dan LejaMeyer and some of Brian's other friends. Dan spotted us and came over to update us on what was going on. Dan had the gist of the events that occurred, but over the next twenty-four hours, others—including Dena—would provide additional details that allowed me to piece together a more complete picture of everything that happened prior to their arrival at Sacred Heart Hospital.

The family had been coming back from Seattle where they'd attended a family reunion on Brian's side. It was around nine o'clock – late enough in August for twilight to be fully settled in. They were about six miles east of Washtucna, a small town of about 200 people that abuts against Washington State Highway 26, a two-lane strip that traverses through the desolate eastern desert region. Brian had seated himself in the front passenger seat while he let Amber drive their minivan. Amber was Brian and Dena's second oldest daughter. She had recently gotten her driver's license and had demonstrated to Brian that she was a good driver, so good that Brian had let her helm the wheel on the streets of downtown Seattle the week before.

Situated in the minivan's middle seat were Dena and their youngest daughter, Alicia. Ashley, their oldest, was stretched out in the very back, trying to catch some sleep before reporting to work on the graveyard shift at the paper mill in Lewiston. She was four days from wrapping up a summer student job there before heading off to college in fall as a freshman.

Amber was doing fine under the watchful eyes of her dad when all of a sudden a deer jumped out onto the road. Amber swerved into the other lane to avoid hitting it, but then she faced another vehicle coming at them in the opposite direction. She swerved again and the combined swings in inertia caused the van to flip and roll about six times down a steep embankment into a ravine.

Ashley had not been wearing a seat belt and was thrown from the car. She landed on some rocks, breaking her back but not impacting the spinal cord. Amber had a hurt shoulder and some cuts but was able to walk around. Dena sustained some bumps and bruises and collected several small shards of glass in her hand, while Alicia's only bruises were from the seat belt restraint across her upper torso.

It was Brian who took the major brunt of impact. Brian's neck was broken and the right side of his skull was crushed, severing an artery on his brain. It took a while for the emergency crews to get to the accident site, since the nearest hospital was in Colfax, a farm town of less than 3,000 people about forty-four miles away from the crash site. But the assistance from travelers coming up on the scene was immediate. Several of them gathered around the family and prayed and tended to the injuries as best they could. One of them played a harmonica, which Dena later admitted caused a strange mixture of bewilderment, comfort, and amusement.

"What are you doing," Dena asked the harmonica player.

"I'm playing hymns," the woman replied.

The emergency crews arrived and extracted Brian from the wreckage and transported him and Ashley to Colfax. As word of the accident reached the members of Brian's church, they abandoned whatever they had been doing that evening and made the hour or so drive to Colfax. They were quick to learn that the hospital there was not equipped to handle injuries as severe as Brian's, and were supportive of Dena's decision to have him air-lifted to Spokane, where the medical facilities offered more advanced options for treatment.

The flight never happened. Shortly after that decision, a severe front of storms moved quickly into the area, bringing bomb-bursts of lightening and high winds, and the skies were too agitated to safely fly a helicopter. The only recourse was to transport Brian by ambulance. They decided to treat Ashley in Spokane too so she rode alongside her dad, while the church family followed behind, taking Dena and the other two girls with them. Along the way Dena began insisting that someone get a hold of me to tell me to get to the hospital, which Dan and Keesha finally succeeded in doing.

"Now here's the strangest part," Dan said, grabbing my arm and pulling me close to him. "Dena was riding with Todd and Keesha and she was rambling most of the trip. I mean, she would say something totally out of place, or worry about something that was just not important. It was like she was in shock."

I nodded. "I understand. I would be in shock, too."

"Who wouldn't? Anyway, Keesha was trying to say whatever she could to comfort Dena. But then Dena fell silent for a few moments, then sat up and started speaking clearly. She said, 'I smell him. He's holding my face. He's talking to me. He says it's going to be ok. He says to take care of the girls.'"

An awe-struck chill shook my soul. I held my breath for a moment before emitting a deep and throaty-sounding, "Whoa!"

Just then a hospital volunteer worker emerged onto the scene and urged us to assemble in one of the ICU waiting rooms. I think there were about fourteen of us in all—some, like me, with their spouses— and we settled apprehensively into the chairs that surrounded the walls of a small rectangular room. Through my association with Brian, I knew most of the people there, although some not very well. What struck me was that with the exception of Debbie and me, all of them were members of the Lewiston First Church of the Nazarene, where Brian and his family worshipped regularly on Sunday morning and fellowshipped frequently in various capacities throughout the week.

What a strong testimony to the brother and sisterhood in Christ to see so many of Brian and Dena's fellow church members here together in this small room, more than a hundred miles away from home and at such a late hour of the night. I marveled at this tangible demonstration of love and support and at that moment wanted so badly to be a part of their church, even though I knew it was not feasible with me living in Spokane. *But wasn't I a part of that church already?* I wondered. *Really, what is the church?*

CHURCH

We raced across the Imperial Gulch trailhead parking lot to the Xterra as the rain continued to assail us. Working quickly, we removed our gear and ditched it onto the backseat before loading our bikes onto the carrier rack. Then we hopped inside the Xterra and slammed the doors shut against the hurricane-like deluge. Within seconds the windows fogged up, obliterating the soggy view outside.

I fired up the engine and turned the heater on full blast, except nothing but frigid air came out of the vents. That coupled with the lingering chill from the icy shower caused our bodies to shiver convulsively, but we stoically waited for the circulating air to heat up enough to penetrate our sodden and muddy clothes and warm our core. Slowly, a clear arc inched its way upward along the windshield from the defrosters, and in time I could see well enough to take off for Ketchum so we could look for a place that would fix Brian's bike. Still, visibility wasn't that great, as the wipers swished back and forth like a pair of crazed metronomes, thrashing furiously to cast off the buckets of water sloshing against the windshield.

"Maybe it's good that we did turn around," Brian conceded. "As wet as we are and as cold as it is we could have been at risk of getting hypothermia."

"That didn't occur to me," I replied. "But that's a good point. Really, all I was thinking about was that we needed to get your bike fixed."

"Look at the bright side," Brian commented as we turned onto the main road leading back to town. "It can't get much worse than this."

"That's for sure," I voiced with certainty. Brian was the kind of man who was eternally optimistic. I admired that attitude and would ultimately come to appreciate just how much it influenced my outlook on distressing matters. I thought about his words and concluded that Brian was right—there really was no way I could get more miserable than my current condition. That's when I noticed that things were at least starting to improve already. The Xterra was providing respite from the downpour and the output from the heater was starting to warm me up pretty well. I began to relax, thinking that the day was not over yet and we would have another opportunity for singletrack Nirvana.

The pounding rain stopped by the time we rolled into Ketchum. We found a bike shop and parked in the back, and Brian unracked his bike and took it inside to the mechanic that was working there that morning. The mechanic looked over the bike for several minutes, while Brian explained what happened, referring to his bike as a "Costco special," the term he used to describe his bike whenever somebody asked him what kind it was. I started feeling bad for him as I realized he must have felt embarrassed for having to take a discount warehouse bike into a shop where many of the bicycles on display sported six, seven, and eight thousand dollar price tags.

"Well, you need more than just a new derailleur," the mechanic intoned when he finished his inspection. "Not only are your brake pads worn but the brake arms are warped."

"Well, it's a Costco special…"

The mechanic jumped right onto that refrain. "That's the point. These bikes aren't built for the kind of riding you do and that's why the components are not holding up."

"Well, I don't want to spend a lot of money…"

The mechanic interrupted again, not in a rude way, but seemingly driven by a passion for making everything right. "The outside of your front shifter is cracked, too, and both the cables are worn."

"…I just need to get it fixed enough so I can finish riding this weekend," Brian continued. "I don't want to put a lot of money into fixing up a Costco special."

I watched Brian squirm as the mechanic started explaining why he also needed a new stem. The price tag for this repair kept escalating with each component the mechanic named, but ultimately the "Costco special" refrain became Brian's out from impoverishment, as he firmly asserted that he did not want to throw good money after bad and just wanted to get his bike functional for a couple more rides. "Especially since I'm going to be buying a new bike soon anyway," he concluded.

That was the first I'd ever heard Brian mention he wanted to get a new bike. In retrospect, I think he made that decision right there in the bike shop. All it took was him hearing just how bad a shape his bike was in and how unsuitable it was for the type of riding he liked to do.

The mechanic got to work fixing just the derailleur, and when the repair was finished, Brian forked over his credit card to cover the $190 cost and we left back to the campsite, munching down on some Costco muffins along the way (seriously—both of our families purchased a lot of stuff from Costco). The muffins were giant calorie bombs, but calories were just what we needed. Besides, they tasted great with bananas and peanut butter and jelly sandwiches and would provide some sorely needed carbohydrates to fuel our next ride

You'd think we'd head back to do the Greenhorn Trail/Imperial Gulch loop, but the mechanic had sold Brian on another trail while he was watching him repair the derailleur. Brian relayed the trail description to me in between giant munches of food. Access to the trailhead started on a forest service road very close to where we were staying, and it promised to provide an exciting section of singletrack that would deposit us back down the mountain close to the campsite. In light of the convenience of the trail's location and how much time we had left that day to ride, it seemed like a good option to take.

On the way back to the campground I noticed a white building housing a hot springs off to the west side of the highway. I wondered if we would be able to plan some time to visit there, and I was glad I'd brought along my swim trunks in case we did. Shortly after that we pulled up into the campground and parked in front of the tent, hurrying inside so we could change out of our damp clothes. It was a fairly large tent with a somewhat flattened top that turned out to have a single leak in it. I had beaten the odds by placing my gym bag with all my clothes directly underneath the leak before leaving that morning. I inventoried the contents and found that the rain had saturated everything except for the swim trunks, which were bone dry.

Brian's clothes were untouched and he had packed enough to loan me a shirt and some socks. We changed out of our wet threads, finished gearing up, then biked our way through the campground onto the Harriman Trail, an all-season, multi-use strip that paralleled Idaho Highway 75, the road between Ketchum and Galena. After pedaling about a mile we reached the forest service road that led to the trailhead for the singletrack at the top of the mountain. Heading west, we rode the first three miles over flat terrain before turning off into another forest service road that marked the beginning of our ascent up the mountain.

From that point on it seemed like we would never stop climbing. Overall it was not a very steep grade, but it just went on and on and on with little variation in the surrounding landscape. The tedium seemed to heighten every physical aspect I was experiencing: somewhat belabored breathing, tingling hands and fingers, the light thump of a pulse in my neck and a growing fatigue in my legs. At last we came upon a downhill section of the road and my heart lifted at the thought of being relieved from the incessant and invariable cranking.

The excitement was short-lived as the next turn revealed we had ridden through a saddle and had more climbing to do to reach the summit. Brian and I settled into a numbed silence and pedaled on until we came to a fork in the road. We took the road leading to the left and ended atop a small prominence that provided us a good view over the lay of the land, but not the trailhead. Brian studied the map before declaring we'd made a wrong turn, so we backtracked until we got back on the right road. At around six thirty we finally arrived at the spot on the map where the trailhead was supposed to be, but we saw nothing but an unmarked, barren area.

"Must be a precision error," I conjectured after silently reasoning that the map scale was too small for us to accurately pinpoint where we were exactly.

"Hmmm…the mechanic said it would be right here," Brian said, planting his finger solidly on the map spread out in front of him. "He pointed to this spot. I'm sure of it."

"Let's ride on a little further and look," I suggested, even though doing that felt like we would be heading in the opposite direction of where we were supposed to go.

"Okay," Brian agreed.

We took off and that "little further" dragged on for a bit. Now much further past where Brian thought we needed to go to find the trailhead I saw a path peeling off the side of the forest service road.

"Look!" I shouted. "This has to be it."

"No, that's not it. It's going the wrong way." Brian pulled out the map and continued, his finger jabbing the paper emphatically. "Look here. We want to get on this trail. This trail." Then, gesturing toward the one in front of us, he explained, "This one is going in the opposite direction."

I could see his point, but I wasn't convinced. "But this is the only trail we've seen off this road since we've hit the summit."

"But I'm telling you it's not the trail we want. We need to go back and look again."

"Okay," I said reluctantly, fighting the irrational urge to want to be right about something I knew nothing about.

After about a mile of backtracking I spotted a slight wisp of a brown strip drifting away at an acute angle from the side of the road, almost invisibly. "What do you think about that?" I asked, stopping the bike to study this faint line in the brush more closely.

Brian pulled up alongside of me and pulled out the map again. His head bobbled back and forth between the map and the landscape for a bit, then he announced, "Yep. This is the one we are looking for. This is the trailhead."

"Are you sure? It looks like it takes us to the foot of that ridge," I said, pointing to a crest that looked to be about three-quarters of the way down the mountain. "But don't we want to end up on the other side of it if we're to get back to the Harriman Trail?"

Brian studied the map one more time, then looked up again. "Yeah, I'm sure."

It just didn't seem right to me, but then again, we had made so many turns and switchbacks during our climb that I could have easily gotten confused. Besides, Brian was the one who talked to the mechanic to get the low-down on the trail, not me, so I figured I should trust his analysis over mine.

"Okay," I conceded, "let's take it, but let's imagine the worst thing that could happen. If we're wrong we get down to the bottom of that ridge and we find out it doesn't take us to where we need to be and we don't know where to go from there to get out. We'll have to bike back up this point, which, assuming the same amount of time it took for us to get here in the first place, would put us back up here at the tail end of twilight. Then we'd go back to the campsite the same way we came up."

I didn't elaborate anymore after that, but I figured Brian would reach the same conclusion that I had. We'd have to coast off the mountain on the forest service road in the dark, probably enduring a good chill along the way. We'd be exhausted, cold, and miserable, but we'd make it back.

If Brian had figured that out in his mind, it didn't seem to worry him. He just looked at me and nodded his head. Either those adverse consequences were trivial to him, or he was so sure of his bearings that he knew we wouldn't have to face that potential outcome.

So off we went, across what looked like an Alpine meadow, the type of setting where you would expect to encounter a Heidi-like maiden leading a herd of cows. The brown trace of a trail became more pronounced the further downhill we rolled, and ahead of us was the line of a fence slicing through the green. Rising up from the trail to meet the fence was a smooth ramp to ride over. As soon as I saw that my heart quickened in excitement. As loudly as I could, I yelled back at Brian, "You were right! This has to be it! Why else would anybody build a bike ramp over a fence?"

Feeling glad that I had trusted him, I cut loose down the mountain with Brian close behind. Soon the meadow yielded to the forest, and then I lost track of time. We wound through the trees on smooth singletrack, flowing and descending swiftly and in good control as I savored an endorphin-fueled sense of glee, each moment more ecstatic that the last. I remained in a ready crouch, using my legs to absorb the bumps and jumps that unfolded underneath. I could feel my quads start to tighten up, and when I could manage it, I did half-circles around the crankshaft to get a little stretch in them.

Approaching the bottom of the mountain, the smooth and rapid ride turned violent as the trail plunged diagonally down a steep slope, coursing over track that was loose and littered with rocks and large pebbles. My full-suspension Specialized Enduro Pro was only a year old and equipped with disc brakes, a relatively new feature for mountain bikes at the time. Despite having used them a lot already I continued to be amazed at the control they gave me, especially as I made the jittery descent in front of me.

Brian was not so fortunate. He was picking up speed so rapidly that he had to bail out several times, the worn-out caliper brakes on his Costco special being no match for the pull of gravity. When he finally skidded to the bottom of the hill, I could see the side effects of all those controlled crashes onto the stony track—irregularly shaped gashes oozing blood on both his legs.

"Are you all right?" I asked.

"Yeah, but I'm pretty cut up," he stated nonchalantly. Then, a non sequitur, entirely in Brian's character: "Wasn't that ride fantastic!"

"Oh, yeah!" I enthused, glad to see he wasn't in pain and happy to share in the rush of joy from the completed descent. "That was worth every bit of the climb! I had no idea it was going to be that good!"

We high-fived one another before we took off again, this time riding across flat land. Now that the exhilaration from the epic downhill ride was starting to dissipate, I started thinking about practical matters. "You know, we probably should find some way to get those wounds on your legs treated," I said.

"Yeah," Brian sighed, as if he didn't really want to, but knew that he should. "Let's look at the map and try to figure out where we are."

I heard traffic not too far away. "Hear those cars going by?" I asked. "That's got to be the highway to Ketchum, so we have to be close to the Harriman Trail." I was so relieved to hear myself say that, knowing the worst-case scenario I had imagined on top of the mountain was not going to come to pass. If we could make our way to the Harriman Trail, it would be a cinch to get back to the campsite so long as we figured out where we had landed relative to where we'd pitched our tent.

A stream flowing through a deep channel lay before us and the path that we were on continued to unwind alongside of it. Not too far south from where we had bottomed out was a bridge. On the other side was a white building at an elevation somewhat lower than our current position.

"Brian! That building! Look!" I was bursting with excitement. "It's the hot springs! I saw it on the way back from the bike shop this morning! Let's go!"

Brian's face lit up. "Just what the doctor ordered!" he exclaimed, and took off toward the bridge like a horse bolting out of the gate at the start of the Kentucky Derby.

I hopped on the bike and started pedaling as fast as I could to catch up when suddenly—and unexpectedly—both legs locked up with horrific, rock-hard cramps. It was as if I had laid eyes on Medusa, but instead of turning completely into stone, I had only been afflicted from the waist down. I howled like a wounded animal and jumped off my bike, my legs locked as straight as a pair of two-by-fours.

Brian stopped. "What's wrong?" he asked, turning back to look my way.

"Cramps. Bad ones!" I answered through clenched teeth. "Keep going. We need to get to the hot springs."

Brian turned back around and started pedaling again, but the only way I could move was by swinging my hips from side to side and letting my petrified appendages flop forward the way you'd expect Frankenstein to move. The pain was excruciating and I thought I was going to collapse on the ground and not be able to move at all, but the thought of having to bend my legs to get to the ground frightened me enough to stay upright. I forced myself to trudge onward, believing the thermal waters at the hot springs were the only chance I had for relief.

We made it to the bridge, and on the other side was a gate, which we had to throw our bikes over before clambering through. I probably could have used some help, but I didn't want to appear weak, even though I was feeling like I couldn't walk another inch. Now we were on the dirt road that led to the white building housing the hot springs, and the slope was downhill from there, so I stood on one of the bike pedals and used a stiff-legged kick to help keep me rolling toward the destination, kind of like a kid on a scooter. I began to tolerate the pain better, knowing relief was not far away.

At last we made it to the entrance of the hot springs. I heard voices inside and reached for the doorknob to go in but it wouldn't turn. Tacked to the locked door was a small sign showing the hours of operation being from ten to seven daily. I looked at my watch: It was 7:35.

My eager anticipation for relief suddenly sagged, but this was not the time to let a sign have the final say. At that same moment I recalled a parable Jesus told in Luke 11:5-8, about a man pounding on his friend's door at midnight asking for some bread to share with an unexpected house guest who'd just arrived. Crabby at the late night intrusion, the friend first refuses to get up and tells the man to go away. Eventually the friend gets up and gives the man everything he asks for, not because he is his friend, but because of the audacity of making such a request at such an hour.

Emboldened by this story, I began knocking on the door vigorously. "There's someone in there. Can you hear them?"

Brian nodded, and in less than a minute a man looking to be in his mid-twenties opened the door.

I tried to be polite, but I don't think it masked my desperation, and it certainly didn't keep me from rambling. "Hi. I know you are closed but I'm hoping that you could make an exception and let us in anyway. We just got through mountain biking and my friend got cut-up pretty badly and needs to wash his wounds and I'm in a lot of pain from leg cramps that the hot springs would help me get over. We won't be any trouble, just need a place to get washed up and soak. I'll pay you twice whatever it costs for going out of your way to let us in. Please. We are both hurting pretty badly."

I was one hundred percent convinced I needed the healing warmth from the hot springs to cure my present infirmity, but I feared my request would be rejected. I'd become jaded from hearing too many anecdotes of people blindly following rules to the letter of the law and not looking beyond the rules to confront and remedy the needs of their fellow human beings. I thought for sure the young man would be one of those types of people and was going to be a stickler on observing the hot spring's business hours. Or maybe my fear stemmed from a simple case of projection. I mean, what would I do if two strange men showed up at my doorstep, dirty, sweaty, bleeding and leg-locked, begging me to let them come into my home so they could use my shower and bathtub?

My brain raced frenetically as I mentally rehearsed what to say next when the young man turned us away, but what he ended up uttering left me speechless. "Come on in. We'll be here for a while. We're teaching kayak lessons in the big pool, but you can get in the shallow end."

I couldn't believe it! I stood there, blinking my wide-eyes for a moment until a sense of gratitude washed over me and I started gushing out all kinds of expressions of thanks. We passed through the door quickly and went directly to the counter. I retrieved my wallet from my CamelBak, ready to plunk down double the admission fee as I had promised. The pricelist posted on a bulletin board behind the counter showed two dollars and fifty cents for adults, so I pulled out two fives to cover the cost for both of us.

"No, that's ok," the young man insisted. "Just two-fifty each is all you need pay."

I took back one of the two fives I'd handed over and glanced again at the bulletin board. Something unexpected had caught my eye when I first looked at the pricelist, and there it was again: the word, "church." It was part of a larger sign, below the price list, that explained church services were held at the hot springs every Sunday morning and evening, along with the starting times. There was a mid-week service as well, also in the evening. "Hmmm," I murmured, pondering the thought of a hot springs and a church coexisting in the same building.

Brian and I proceeded into a clean and bright locker room and wasted no time jumping into a hot and soapy shower. Once we were clean enough to enter the pool, we dressed back into our mountain-biking shorts and exited the locker room. Sure enough, a kayaker was in the deep end with an older man standing on the edge of the pool giving him instructions. We eased into the shallow end, away from the two men, and allowed the analgesic heat to seep into our muscles and joints. I exulted in the healing waters as every last vestige of stiffness from my cramps dissolved. I was restored.

I thought I had banged on the door of the hot springs, but the grace shown to me by the young man convinced me I really had banged on the door of the church. It made me think: *I want my church to be a beacon of hope, like a white building that's easily seen from a distance. I want it to be a place where those that hurt and suffer can seek relief. Where grace welcomes strangers into the healing waters sourced in the blood that Jesus shed for all on the cross at Calvary. Where his body—the church—is equipped to respond to the needs of others in selfless love utilizing the various gifts he bestows upon it. Where we are restored as children of God, whole and complete.*

Who would ever think a rambunctious mountain bike ride followed by a visit to a hot springs would teach such a lesson?

THE PROGNOSIS

August 3, 2014

I surveyed the faces in the ICU waiting room, trying to recall names of the people that looked familiar but whom I hadn't seen in a long time. Someone escorted Dena in and helped her to a seat on the opposite side of the room where Debbie and I were sitting. No sooner had she settled in when she started recounting her supernatural encounter with Brian on the drive to Spokane. Her voice, though plaintive, communicated urgency and gravity.

It was one thing to hear this story from Dan, but to have Dena bear witness in the first person was utterly astonishing. I whipped out my phone and transcribed her words into my notebook app so I would have an accurate record of what she said. Watching the text form across the tiny screen made me concentrate more on what she was saying, helping me to realize that Brian had already passed on to the other side. Sure, his body was still in the ICU, and the medical staff were doing their best to keep him alive, but it seemed apparent now that his soul had left this earthly realm and entered into the dimension that encompasses Paradise. None of us alive can be sure of what that's like unless, like the apostle Paul recounts in 2 Corinthians 12:3-4, we get caught up into it.

Just then the waiting room door opened. The doctor on call edged in and took the nearest seat. We all fell silent as we riveted our attention to him.

"Brian's neck is broken and he has severe head trauma," he began, confirming the injuries we already knew about. "We ran an MRI and it showed he has a blood clot on the brain, and there's a large amount of swelling around that area. The oxygen levels in his blood tested low when he arrived here from Colfax and we found that his nose and nasal passages were full of blood, which impeded his respiration and led to the low levels of oxygen. He won't survive unless we operate on him, but even then there's no guarantee of saving him," the doctor flatly stated.

The room was so quiet that I could hear myself swallow through what felt like a thickening throat. The doctor continued, "The neck break is severe enough that even if he survives the surgery, there is a strong chance he would be in a wheel chair the rest of his life, unable to take care of himself."

I noticed the doctor made no mention of the prognosis for the recovery of his mental faculties. Being somewhat familiar with traumatic head injuries, I reasoned that the severe head trauma and lengthy exposure to low oxygen levels did not bode well for the future health of his brain, either. Nothing the doctor had said so far offered any hope.

"I need a decision on whether we should operate to try to save him or to let nature take its course," the doctor declared, not only challenging us to think the unthinkable but also raising the specter of our own fleeting mortality, currently personified in Brian's tenuous hold on life.

Considering how much medical technology had advanced in my lifetime, I thought to myself, *Fifty years ago this wouldn't have been a decision anyone would have to make.* Before all the breakthroughs in the treatment of devastatingly traumatic injuries, what other course did the medical community have to offer to the families of accident victims except to admit that the life was in God's hands from that point forward?

As I silently pondered the question, the doctor turned to Dena and asked, "Is your husband an organ donor?"

"Yes," she affirmed.

He nodded his head slowly. "If there is the decision to let nature take its course, then there would need to be a discussion about donating his organs," he informed her, as if he knew just how poor Brian's chances of survival were but needed to communicate indirectly what he thought Dena's response should be. Rising from his chair, the doctor said, "I'll leave you alone so you can think through this with your friends."

Dena was obviously distraught, but who wouldn't be, given that she faced the most difficult decision she'd ever been confronted with in her entire life. Despite her distress, I detected a calm demeanor projecting from somewhere deep inside that I could only explain as coming from an unshakable and abiding faith in God. Perhaps she felt that he was still in control of the situation, no matter how grim it had become. At any rate, Dena began to deliberate on the two options before her, freely sharing her thoughts with us as she weighed out the potential consequences of each course of action. After a few minutes she said, "It's strange but two weeks ago Brian and I were talking about this and he said if he ever got into this kind of situation then he didn't want anything done to be kept alive."

Knowing Brian as well as I did, it seemed totally in character for him to make such a declaration. I had a sense the other men in the room recognized this fundamental truth about him too, given how strongly they knew his life was about living it fully and serving others with an almost boundless physicality. I thought to myself, *Perhaps Brian had a premonition about what was going to happen and he was addressing what to do ahead of time.*

Maybe Dena was thinking the same thing. At any rate, she seemed on the verge of making the decision to let events proceed when her voice began to crack with doubt, telegraphing a profound fear of letting Brian go without doing something—anything—to try to keep him alive. That calm center of faith that was helping her hold together had disappeared, and her anxiety over what to do appeared to be tearing her apart inside. "Help me!" she pleaded. "Tell me what I should do!"

Dena's in spiritual warfare, I thought to myself. How else to explain the suddenly transition from being rooted in her faith to becoming overwhelmed with discouragement? I felt a tremendous flash of anger toward whatever minion of Satan had swooped in to prey upon her, given the gravity of the circumstances into which she had been thrust. I struggled on how to speak out at this moment to combat this evilness, but before I could resolve what to do Aaron Middleton, the youth pastor at the Nazarene Church and Brian's cross-fit training partner, spoke up. "Everyone, listen up," he commanded with urgent authority. "We need to pray. Let's join hands."

Thank you Lord, I muttered under my breath. *Prayer is what we need to dispel this evil.* I began to listen for what words Aaron would lead us in, knowing that prayer at critical moments can be challenging to say the least, and also wise to the fact that what we pray for in those moments doesn't always get answered the way we expect.

PRAYER

"What trail do you want to ride first?" I asked as I lifted my bike off the rack on the rear of the Xterra. Even though it was a weeknight, Brian and I were psyched to take advantage of the extended daylight from the summer solstice and schedule an after work road trip to Moscow Mountain for a good three hours of trail riding. There were certainly plenty of trails to choose from.

"Let's do Rock and a Hard Place," Brian replied. "I've been wanting to try it out."

It was a relatively new trail, and neither one of us had ridden it yet. "Sounds good to me," I said.

We mounted our bikes and prayed for our ride ahead, then Brian took the lead and I followed close behind. The initial run of the trail moved pretty fast before it started twisting and turning though the forest. Then the descent flattened out slightly as the trail approached the rock that begat its namesake. Brian flew over the rock without hesitation, dropping off the ledge and landing with a hard thump, his wheels wobbling slightly as he regained his balance and began pedaling onward.

I pulled up to the rock but stopped short of making the drop. Down below, the thick canopy blanketed the trail in dark and foreboding shadows, adding to my pause to continue. Even though it wasn't that high, it looked like a difficult drop to make, and I was afraid I wouldn't be able to manage it. But I wanted to do it, badly. As I often do when I face difficult situations, I started praying, but this silent prayer was a lot more fervent than the one we prayed out loud right before we took off. It went something like this: *Dear God, please give me courage and help me to make this drop and land safely.* I repeated it several times.

I backed up a few yards, then took off straight for the center of the rock. Making drops like this may be routine for some, but it wasn't a feature I was used to encountering on the trails I usually rode. That lack of experience is probably why I got careless and let my front wheel get below me after it cleared the edge. When the wheel touched down the front suspension compressed the full length while the rear wheel flipped upward, sending me soaring off the bike.

I landed face down, splayed-limbed, the front of my helmet plowing a narrow furrow onto the surface of the trail. It was a hard hit, and I felt a tightness and tingling in my neck. I couldn't move, almost as if all my muscles were frozen. Now a new and more urgent fear gripped me: what if I had broken my neck and was paralyzed? I told myself not to panic, but I couldn't move, couldn't speak, couldn't get myself pushed up off the ground and back to my feet.

Try something easy, I thought to myself. *Check the fingers on your right hand.*

I lifted up the fingers of my right hand one at a time, and released them back to the earth, then several more times, all at once.

Ok, left hand.

Same pattern as before, until I could coordinate them like I was playing four consecutive notes on a piano.

Legs…check the legs. Right leg first. Start with the toes.

I wiggled my toes in my trail boot, then flexed my ankle, pushing back the point of the shoe.

Left leg.

I lifted it up off the ground, flexing the knee, and curling the toes at the same time.

Ok! I'm ok! The hit must have just stunned me!

The sweeping relief that I was not going to be a quadriplegic instantly energized me. I jumped up off the ground and started scraping off the dirt that clung to my clothes and skin, checking for any injuries as I whisked the debris away. My left elbow hurt slightly, so I twisted my arm toward me and looked at the backside and saw a large, bright red scrape.

Well, that explains the pain there, I reasoned. *Nothing that a little spit can't take care of.* I formed a pearl-sized amount of saliva in my mouth and dribbled it onto the wound, my standard way of treating minor cuts and scrapes on the trail.

I hopped back on my bike and started pedaling as fast as I could, thinking I was way behind Brian now and needing to cover a lot of trail to catch up. I met him more quickly than I thought, as he had started backtracking after he'd stopped to wait for me and realized I wasn't catching up with him soon enough. I told him I'd wiped out, but was okay. I didn't mention the prayer, nor did I tell him how fearful I was laying there on the ground moments after the crash. Instead I urged that we get going again. Daylight was burning and we had more riding to do.

The rest of the evening was pure joy. On every subsequent trail we rode we reveled in perfect track: firm, with just the right amount of tack to keep your lines true and to let you take turns faster than you could any other time of the year. Soon summer's heat would bake out the surface moisture left behind from the snow melt and spring rains, and all the pounding of knobby tires would pulverize the trail surfaces, leaving a brown talcum powder deposit that makes your wheels feel like they're smearing the ground instead of rolling over it. Knowing the trail conditions were not going to get any better than what we were experiencing that evening amplified our enjoyment.

We saved our favorite trail for last – Contour Trail, a smooth and fast strip of dirt that made a long and fast cut across the profile of the mountain slope. It was a little after nine o'clock now, as dusky light accumulated in the western sky, making the heavily canopied sections of the trail feel like tunnels. But we knew the trail by heart, down to the individual bumps and rocks, and we flew like crop dusters swooping toward the ground, captivated by the speed and flow of the descent as we hurtled through the forest in reckless abandonment.

We always savored the ride on Contour Trail, but this evening it was sheer bliss, a flawless union of man, dirt, and machine.

"That's got to be the best we've ever ridden!" I declared to Brian at the end of the run, as laughter bubbled out of us like water from an artesian well.

"I can't believe how fast that was!" he exclaimed. "I was flying around those turns!"

I pulled out my GPS unit. "Wow…I'm showing a top speed of twenty-seven miles per hour!"

"I wish we could do it again," Brian lamented, cognizant of the rapidly fading light.

"Yeah, me too." I sighed, aware that my ecstatic gulps of breath and sense of exuberance were starting to subside. "We better head back to the Xterra."

Brian hesitated before responding, as if signaling that we needed to soak up the glory of the moment for just a little longer. Finally, he said, "Red-eye?" It was his signature catchphrase that prompted us to resume riding.

"Ready," I chuckled, always getting a kick out of his word play.

We turned our wheels back toward the mountaintop and began the climb back to where I'd parked. The encroaching darkness was about to completely engulf us when we arrived, spurring us to remove our gear hurriedly and get our bikes in position to mount on the rack hitched to the back of the Xterra. I picked up my bike and stretched out my left arm to maneuver it over the first three cradles in the rack, but my left arm didn't work the way I wanted it to. Instead it remained locked in a biking position; that is, the somewhat bent position the arm assumes when it grips the handlebars.

"Uh, oh," I said to Brian. "There's something wrong with my arm." It was a matter-of-fact statement, with a level of alarm in my voice low enough to suggest I'd only noticed a small scratch.

"What is it?" he asked, moving in closer to examine it.

"I can't bend it."

"How'd that happen?"

"I don't know. It must have been when I wiped out. It's not hurting…"

Brian offered what anyone would say looking at such an abnormal situation. "Maybe you better get that looked at."

"Yeah, probably should," although I didn't think it was something I needed to go to the emergency room for, at least not right away.

We climbed into the Xterra and took off for home. Halfway there, my elbow started hurting, but only slightly at first. Just like after every other lengthy bout of riding, I was filled with an infusion of endorphins, which usually made me feel euphoric for hours afterwards. Tonight they were numbing the pain, but as the endorphins continued to subside on the ninety-minute trip home, the hurt grew. By the time I'd dropped Brian off at his home in Lewiston and crossed over the Snake River to Clarkston, I felt pretty sure I was headed for a difficult night, once I completely came down from the wide-eyed excitement I still felt from the incredible riding experience we'd shared that evening. Eventually I made it to bed and slept for a while, but the pain caused me to awaken a couple of hours later and sleeping was off and on for the rest of the night after that.

I called my orthopedist the next day for an appointment but had to wait three days until I could get in to see him. I figured it was worth it as he was already familiar with my elbow, as I had sought his advice nine months earlier upon the recommendation of my chiropractor, who'd seen me in the gym holding a pair of hundred-pound dumbbells and had noticed that my left arm was not straightening out under that load. The orthopedist had done a thorough exam and medical history review and had concluded then that my elbow had some significant structural issues that developed from an injury I had there when I was five years old, which was not properly treated: arthrosis (degenerative joint disease similar to arthritis), osteophyte formation (bone spurs) and sclerosis (thickening and hardening of the bones).

So, there were already problems with my left elbow before that evening on Moscow Mountain. Now, nine months later and another round of x-rays, my orthopedist concluded that my crash on Moscow Mountain had added fractures of some of those osteophytes plus the coronoid process (the triangular part of the ulna that protrudes into the elbow joint) to that list of maladies.

So, I got a robotic-looking elbow brace, enrolled in physical therapy, and began the rehabilitation process. When I wasn't being manipulated directly by the therapist, the exercises were much like what I would call classical weight lifting for the biceps and triceps muscles around the elbow joint. Over time most of my mobility came back, and I went on with my life, the only indication of ever having an issue being whenever I suited up for a mountain bike ride. I had a new piece of gear to strap on—a high-impact plastic protector that I could Velcro around the elbow joint of my left arm. It was one piece of an array of protective gear that downhill mountain bikers were quite familiar with, but it was new to me.

Another season of riding came and went, then suddenly in 2007 there was a new training movement that sprung up out of nowhere, one that we just had to check out: CrossFit. Wow! We were so impressed! Brian started doing the workouts of the day at five-thirty every morning, while I often improvised my own workout whenever I could fit it into my schedule. Sometimes Brian and I would meet up at the pool and invent what we called Navy SEAL workouts, nowhere near as grueling as what the real heroes went through during Hell Week but still laden with an intensity that left us sprawled out on the concrete deck, wet and exhausted. I got less and less interested in the normal gym routines and eventually decided no more classical weight lifting for me. CrossFit was the real thing, the real way to train!

That enthusiasm and commitment to CrossFit continued up to summer 2008, when I was no longer living in Clarkston. Work had transferred me to Spokane, but I had lived there independently for seven months while my wife Debbie and youngest daughter Emily stayed in Clarkston so Emily wouldn't have to finish the last six months of her senior year in a new high school. I was still improvising CrossFit workouts and Brian and I were regularly comparing notes about what we were up to via email.

Emily graduated and summer came, and we were about two weeks away from moving into our new home in Spokane when I came across some sad news: the only true mentor I ever had at work passed away after a fight with cancer. His name was John Bacon, and he was the vice president of strategic planning for the same forest products company both Brian and I worked for. I got to work with John when I was asked to take over strategic planning for the pulp and paperboard business division and he taught me more about critical thinking than anybody I ever knew, helping me to overcome intellectual laziness in thought processes where I didn't even know it existed. Something I didn't know about John when I worked with him was that he was a fellow brother in Christ, but that would become evident to me during his wake, which I had planned to attend on the first Friday evening in August of 2008.

Paying my last respects to John was an occasion that called for dressing up. I hadn't worn a tie in I didn't know how long, and didn't even have one in the closet at my temporary living quarters. I ran by a thrift shop after work and picked out a tie that went with my blue blazer, which fortunately I *had* brought with me.

As I started getting dressed to go to the wake, to my utter surprise, my left elbow would not bend inward enough to reach the top button of my dress shirt so I could fasten it. I tried and tried to make it bend, but it wouldn't. At a certain point in flexion, my elbow froze. I even put a towel against my forearm and leaned it into a doorjamb, using my body-weight to force the elbow joint to bend so I could reach my neck, but to no avail. I couldn't even fasten the top button just using one hand, so I tried a different dress shirt, only to I realize (for the first time ever) that all my dress shirts had a horizontal hole for the top button and vertical holes for all the other ones, making it impossible for me to manipulate the button single-handedly through the top hole.

Now stewing in frustration and disbelief, I sat down on the side of the bed, baffled at discovering this infirmity. How could this have happened without me noticing it? I thought back to all the trouble I'd had with my left elbow after the accident, and all the work I did with weights to rehab it. Why, then, does it freeze like it does, kind of like the night it froze when I had the wreck on Moscow Mountain?

Then it occurred to me: I had stopped the traditional weight lifting movements that I always used to do around the elbow joint—the same bicep and triceps exercises and I had done during rehab for my elbow—and had switched to CrossFit workouts. When CrossFit workouts did use weights, they were more for powerlifting and Olympic lifting, multiple-joint movements versus isolation work for the muscle groups around the elbow. It was the traditional weight lifting work that had made my arm mobile again and had kept it that way—that is, until I abandoned it for CrossFit.

Feeling totally discouraged, I sagged forward, trying to put my head in my hands, only to fail at that, as I couldn't get the elbow to bend enough to allow the left hand to meet my forehead—another shock. As I sat on the bed, struggling against a slide into despondency, my mind drifted back the events right before the injury occurred on that evening on Moscow Mountain. I remembered the prayer I made before going over the ledge, and I could not understand how God could hear such a simple prayer like that and have the long-term result be a physical deformation. "How could this happen?" I plaintively yelled out.

My bewilderment would have probably turned to despair had I not been so time-conscious and realized I needed to get going to make the memorial service in time. I pressured myself to snap out of my ruminations and went back to dealing with the issue with my shirt and tie. I decisively left the top unbuttoned and slid the slip knot of my tie tightly against my neck to hide the fact that my collar button was unfastened. Then I hurried out the door.

The funeral home was fairly crowded when I got there, so I sat near the back row. The casket with John's remains was opened in the center of the aisle at front, and I could see the ravages of cancer in his wispy white hair and fragile face—not the same vital, dynamic, and energetic looking man I remembered from when I worked with him. I averted my gaze from then on, not wanting to corrupt my better memories of John with the reality of what that evil disease had done.

I took comfort in knowing that the next time I would see John, I would see him in his resurrected body, for this is how the Apostle Paul states it in 2 Corinthians 5:1-5:

"Our body is like a house we live in here on earth. When it is destroyed, we know that God has another body for us in heaven. The new one will not be made by human hands as a house is made. This body will last forever. Right now, we cry inside ourselves because we wish we could have our new body which we will have in heaven. We will not be without a body. We will live in a new body. While we are in this body, we cry inside ourselves because things are hard for us. It is not that we want to die. Instead, we want to live in our new bodies. We want this dying body to be changed into a living body that lasts forever. It is God Who has made us ready for this change. He has given us His Spirit to show us what He has for us" (NLV).

Two years later I would think back to that memorial service and Paul's words. I had signed up to go see a specialist in Spokane to see if there was anything that could be done to repair my elbow and restore its full functionality. Unfortunately, there wasn't. It was basically unfixable, and an artificial elbow joint was out of the question. *Oh, well,* I thought as I faced the truth of my situation, *just like John, one day I'll have a resurrection body in Heaven and I won't have to worry about this elbow any more.*

I wonder if God met me on that ledge on Moscow Mountain that evening in 2005 when I prayed to Him? Would being in His presence explain why I fell prostrate to the ground, unable to move or speak? Did he cripple my elbow, just like He wrestled with Jacob and crippled his hip (see Genesis 32:24-30)? That elbow reminds me to stop giving so much attention to this perishable, fleshly body that houses my soul. It reminds me that one day all that's wrong with me—physically and spiritually—will be wiped away and I will be restored with a glorious, indestructible body; sanctified and in the holy presence of Jesus.

It seems to me that God has granted me everything I prayed for that evening on Moscow Mountain, but not the way I thought. I've cleared the ledge of death and landed safely in the arms of a Savior who will help me continue on the present journey until I meet him face to face. Sure, it's not the outcome I prayed for, but isn't the promise of the eternal outcome infinitely better than the momentary one I had wished for before going over the rock that evening?

DIFFICULT MOMENTS

August 3, 2014

As Aaron prayed in the waiting room, he spoke earnestly before the Lord. The next few moments were powerful as his prayer dispelled the dark forces that had descended and ushered in the quieting presence of the Holy Spirit. I felt a unity with the souls in that room that made it seem as if we were a single entity approaching the holy throne of God.

The main thrust of Aaron's prayer was asking for wisdom to help guide Dena to the right decision on whether to operate on Brian in an attempt to save his life, or to let nature take its course. I felt comforted by that request, knowing how many times God had honored my petitions for wisdom in tough situations, yet none as trying as the one now facing Dena. We said amen, and the composure achieved during the prayer remained with us as Dena resumed the deliberations around the difficult decision facing her, utilizing the inputs of her assembled friends to help ease the burden that had been placed upon her.

It wasn't long before the subject came up around Brian's wishes for what Dena should do if he ever got into an incapacitating situation such as this. I thought it was beyond coincidence that Brian and Dena would have had this conversation so recently. While I couldn't say that Brian had acted upon a premonition about the tragedy that had now befallen his family, I did believe the Holy Spirit had moved him to address this vital question in preparation for this moment. As such, many of us in the room talked about how important it would be to honor Brian's wishes. I knew the folks around me well enough to assert that we all respected the sanctity of life, but it didn't seem fair to Brian to override his expressed wishes just so we could honor that sentiment, especially when we didn't have to live out the consequences of what the prognosis for that life would be like if he survived the surgery—assuming he did survive.

Then again, it seemed to many of us that Brian was already with the Lord, on account of the supernatural experience Dena had with him speaking assurances to her on the way to Spokane from Colfax. Was it possible that Brian's spirit had passed but his body was surviving under the functions of medical support devices? Would a successful surgery call him back from a "near death" experience into a radically different life that was totally out of his character and nature? As it was meant to be, I would never find out the answer to that last question. Dena decided to let nature take its course and to allow Brian's organs to be harvested for those chronically afflicted souls who were awaiting life-changing transplants.

Dena's decision got relayed to the doctor, and shortly after that a different member of the hospital staff came into the room and asked Dena to go with her to begin the necessary paperwork to allow organ donations to proceed. Soon another staff member appeared and requested we move to another waiting room closer to Brian. Dena joined us there when she had completed signing all of the consent forms.

Over the next couple of hours we sat and talked, trying to process all that was happening. Dan LejaMeyer was moving in and out, roving around the hospital in an on-going effort to get updates on what was happening. Whenever he learned something, he returned to give us a briefing. At one point Dena asked Dan if he could get a picture of Brian. Dan went into the ICU and asked the on-duty nurse if he could step into Brian's room to take the photograph. At first she refused, but then the "you look familiar" dialogue broke out and the two of them discovered that she was his pupil when he was a teacher at Clarkston High School. With that realization, she let Dan go in and get the picture. After showing it to Dena, he shared it with others in the room, but not everybody wanted to view it. I looked, and became deeply saddened to see my best friend in such a broken condition.

Brian's other best friend—if you can allow there can be more than one best friend—was in the waiting room, too, and had been on the scene ever since getting the call to come to Colfax. His name was

Jeremy Carr, and he was a lawyer in Lewiston and one of Brian's most consistent CrossFit training partners. Brian and Jeremy were into backcountry skiing the way Brian and I were into mountain biking. I had a pretty good idea of what kind of friend Jeremy was to Brian, given how much Brian told me about the activities they did together. Also, I'd done some things with Jeremy before—mainly mountain biking—but never felt a bond to him like I felt at that moment when I took notice of him in the waiting room. Here, too, was someone who had just lost his best friend, and my empathy for him was immediate. I don't think such unexpressed knowledge is possible between two people without the brotherhood in Christ that we shared.

At one moment nearly everyone had drifted out of the room for various reasons, and Jeremy and I were alone together. With this sudden and unexpected privacy the waiting room became a place of refuge from the onslaught of events, allowing us to reveal the raw hurt and bewildering thoughts that gripped us. As much as we acknowledged the internal pain that we felt, we were acutely aware of how much more Dena must be feeling, so we committed to praying for her, not just for now and the immediate future, but also for the months that were to follow.

Just then Dan LejaMeyer popped back into the room with an announcement. "They're going to let us go in and say our goodbyes to Brian. Dena and the girls first, then the rest of us in groups of two to four."

I turned to Jeremy. "Do you want to go in together when our turn comes?"

"Sure," he nodded in reply.

It wasn't long before we saw Dena, Amber, and Alicia scuffling tentatively alongside a gurney on which Ashley lay, supported by a board, her back injury serious but not life threatening. They pressed close to each other as they shuffled slowly down the hallway toward Brian's room. As they passed, Jeremy and I looked at one another then bowed our heads and together we prayed for them. From there they went in to say their final goodbyes.

To this day I don't know what transpired next, since out of respect for the sanctity and privacy of that moment I never asked. I can easily imagine that it had to be one of the most tender and heartbreaking moments in the entirety of the Johnson family's life together. I found out later that after Dena and the girls had said farewell to their husband and father, Brian's EEG activity ceased and the attending physician declared him brain dead. Somehow, even though he was gone, a spark of his presence had lingered just long enough to give his family solace that the gesture associated with those final moments mattered.

Meanwhile the rest of group had congregated back in the waiting room. A nurse stopped in to inform us that we would still get the opportunity to say goodbye, but we needed to wait while the medical staff could perform some preparatory work related to Brian being an organ donor. Knowing the espresso stand in the hospital commissary had opened for business, Debbie and I went and fetched several cups of freshly brewed coffee for all of us who needed the caffeine. When I had the chance to sit down again, I sipped on the hot and embracing brew and began to review the responses to the several text messages I had sent out earlier that morning.

The first text, explaining what had happened and asking for prayers, had gone out to Doug Weinrich, the minister of servant leadership development at our home church in Spokane, Redeemer Lutheran. Doug had recently moved from Puyallup, Washington, and had only been on the church staff for about a month. During his interview trip the previous fall, I learned that Doug was an avid mountain biker. Hearing that, I made a point to introduce myself and pitch the benefits of moving to the Spokane based on the quality of mountain biking in the region, with special emphasis on Moscow Mountain. Within the short month since he'd been here, I'd mentioned how much I looked forward to getting him down to Moscow Mountain soon and riding with Brian and me, so Doug knew who Brian was when he read that first message I'd sent to him that morning. He'd responded shortly after I'd sent the message, saying he would call me in a little while.

Before I could finish reading the rest of the responses to my text messages, the phone rang. It was Doug, true to his word. Right away he asked me if I wanted him to come out to the hospital. As if by reflex, I started to say, "No, I'll be all right, thanks though." But deep down, I knew those words would ring hollow if I spoke them, and I was ashamed at how readily I was inclined to be superficial—to act like I was so in control that I didn't need someone with ministerial bona fides during one of the most distressing episodes of my life. The truth was, I was not all right, and I needed the strength of another faithful brother in Christ beside me to help me get through the next hour.

"Yes," I answered, relieved that I had spoken the truth.

"I'll be right there," he replied.

Within the next half hour before Doug arrived, the medical staff had completed their prep work necessary for Brian to be an organ donor, and the attending nurse began allowing smaller groups of us to go in and say our goodbyes. Jeremy and I sat and watched as the sad and weeping faces of friends and acquaintances made their way to where Brian's lifeless body lay. Shortly after Doug showed up the nurse told Jeremy and me it was our turn to say goodbye to Brian. Jeremy reached out to Aaron and asked him if he would come with us; likewise, I asked Doug to join as well. Just before the four of us went into the room, Aaron has us pause in the hallway so he could lead us in prayer. We huddled in a tight circle and laid hands on one another's shoulders as Aaron asked God to prepare us for what we were about to do.

Mustering the courage to make that next step to enter into Brian's room seemed as difficult as pushing on the pedal of my mountain bike just before riding over the ledge on the Rock and a Hard Place trail on Moscow Mountain. I may have not been ready emotionally to do this but intellectually I knew I had to see Brian one last time, no matter what he looked like. I needed to say goodbye to him to confront the reality of what was happening and begin the process of closure to the terrible dream-like event in which we were all immersed.

Aaron, Doug, Jeremy, and I gathered around the bed, beholding Brian in a state of existence that we could have never conceived. As soon as I saw his bruised and battered face, distorted even further by the invasive ventilator tube, my heart dropped from my chest to my feet, leaving a vacuum of heavy sorrow in its wake. The ache intensified as remembrances of his naturally radiant and unblemished appearance flashed through my mind in startling contrast to the visage of the man lying recumbent on the hospital bed before me, his body surrounded by a multitude of medical instruments. I let my gaze settle on his soul patch, the only unmarred feature on his disproportionately swollen head.

Truth be told, I had always been secretly afraid something traumatic like this would happen to Brian, not from something as common as a car wreck but from something related to his exploits on the trail. While I had always admired his skill and courage, and had attempted at times to emulate it, I realized there were areas where he went that I could never go. As I stared in bewilderment at his afflicted body, my thoughts flashed briefly back to the event that formed the origin of my secret fear.

COVETING

Not much mountain biking in the summer of 2006. I'd been assigned to take over project management of an over-budget, behind schedule software implementation at a pulp and paper mill in rural southeastern Arkansas. Except for a few weekend trips home, I spent most of the summer confined to the flatlands of the Mississippi Delta. No mountains there to bike on, that's for sure, and I was lucky if I could just find time to squeeze in some type of exercise at all, as the days at the mill were long and challenging.

The technical team completed the installation and startup of the software in the first part of September, and I was able to return home shortly after that. I was eager to get in some much-needed trail adventures before the mountain-biking season ended, so naturally Brian was the first person I approached about doing this. After several email exchanges and phone calls, we came up with a plan to do a weekend in the McCall area, spending one day on a trail we'd never ridden in the Payette National Forest, and the next day trying out the downhill trails at the newly-opened Tamarack Resort, a multimillion-dollar development in Donnelly, Idaho, about thirteen miles south of McCall. It seemed like a good start toward making up for all the fun I'd missed that summer.

Brian let me handle recruiting some other riders to join us, and I contacted several friends but as it turned out only one of them, Carl Strong, could get away to join us that weekend. At the time, Carl was the manager of the Asotin County Family Aquatics Center. We had gotten to know Carl since he had taught Brian, me and about a dozen other men how to play water polo during an eight-week evening class at the aquatics center one winter. One night after class we hung around the pool to chat a bit and got into a discussion about which workout was more intense: water polo or mountain biking. During the discussion Carl revealed he was interested in doing some mountain biking with us so we started reaching out to him to join us on some of our rides.

Brian volunteered to drive and so he picked up Carl and me Friday after work. My neighbor had recommended a trail near Upper Payette Lake just north of McCall called Twenty Mile. Having been to that area before, I knew of some good camping spots on the lake, and we made it there by nightfall, pitching the tent with the help of the headlights from Brian's minivan before settling in for the night.

Sometime after midnight I woke up to the sound of rain falling lightly on the canvas. I could hear the cadence of the soft drops slowly building over the next few hours as I drifted in and out of sleep. As dawn neared, the rain leveled off then stopped. I scrunched more deeply into my sleeping bag and started dozing again, relieved that we wouldn't have to ride in wet weather that morning.

A short time later Brian stirred and then left the tent to fire up the camp stove. Carl and I slowly unraveled our sleeping bags and got dressed in our riding clothes, then went out and hovered around a pan of boiling water, taking turns making instant coffee and instant oatmeal while warming our hands close to the burner. After eating our meager breakfast we hopped into the minivan and took off to find the Twenty Mile trailhead. When we emerged from under the campground's tree canopy onto the main road, we got a good view of the land around us and were surprised to see snow just slightly above our current elevation. We stayed below the snowline until we reached Twenty Mile, where the magical transition from mud to powder occurred just as we rolled our bikes out of the parking lot and faced the wooden sign marking the trail's entrance.

It was the first time riding in snow, and it felt harder than riding in the fine, granular soil of Sand Boulevard, a trail on Moscow Mountain that we seldom rode on account of the sluggish track that its namesake implied. There was no problem making out Twenty Mile's path—a long, linear dimple in the snow blanket with bumpy spots where large stones protruded upward, but moving along that path was difficult. Wads of wet snow packed into the tire treads, sometimes so badly that the wheels became bound against the front fork and stopped turning. We released some of the air pressure in our tires and that seemed to help us move along, so we trudged on for a couple of hours until we reached a small wall of boulders.

"Keep going?" Brian asked after climbing over the array of stones then turning to see Carl and I still standing below.

"I vote we turn back," Carl confessed unabashedly.

"I'm with Carl," I added. "These conditions aren't making this trail that much fun."

"All right," Brian conceded, a tinge of disappointment in his voice.

Even though the ride back was mostly downhill, the descent wasn't much of a payoff for all the work it took to reach that point. We steered our way along the tracks we'd already made, but it still required a lot of work to keep moving. The temperature was steadily rising, and the closer we got to the trailhead the more the snow cover disintegrated. Soon we were traversing a line of mud that ended up coating our bike frames and splattering up on us in a gradient of dirt, our lower extremities looking like we were undergoing some luxury spa treatment while our faces got what looked like random spots of new mole growths.

Back at the minivan, Carl and I commiserated on what a bust the ride was, but Brian remarked he thought it was fun; then again, Brian could usually find something fun in every adventure he undertook, no matter how it turned out. We all agreed we needed to get cleaned up but there were no shower facilities at the Upper Payette Lake campground, so we broke camp and headed into McCall to find a cheap motel with a shower and three beds. We got the former wish, but ended up having to settle for a room with only two beds, so we drew straws to see who slept on the floor.

After we'd all cleaned up and changed, we drove to a laundromat to wash our bike clothes, and then found a do-it-yourself car wash that advertised it could handle RVs. That suited us just fine, as what we really wanted to do was to rinse off our bikes which we'd left fastened in the rack on top of the minivan—adding up to about the same height as an RV. We pulled into the concrete pad and starting feeding the coin box with quarters like a compulsive gambler at a slot machine. There was a small, metal platform with stairs built next to the wall that allowed you to spray the upper area of your RV, and I used that to make sure the bikes got really doused with soap and water. We got the bikes cleaned and used the remaining time to clean Brian's minivan. Afterwards, we drove back into downtown McCall for dinner then walked around before calling it a day and heading back to the motel.

Sunday morning came with a glorious burst of sunshine. Today was the day to make up for yesterday's disappointment (at least for Carl and me), so we wasted no time in checking out of the motel and making the fifteen minute drive down to Donnelly. A prominent sign told us where to turn to the Tamarack Resort, and we wound our way over and around the northern bays of Cascade Lake to the main lodge, past large signs that touted the three phases of development going on at the resort.

We parked and made our way to the rental center where we saw a beefy fleet of fat-tired downhill bikes arrayed in a couple of racks. None of us had ever ridden on a downhill bike before, and Carl and I had already made up our minds to rent one and give it a go. Brian, on the other hand, had decided to use his bike. He'd checked on the rental fees ahead of time and concluded the expenditure was at odds with his current budget. However, once he saw the excitement Carl and I displayed when we started trying out the bikes and talking about the riding possibilities that they held in store for us, Brian changed his mind and decided to rent one as well.

Of course, we also had to rent protective equipment. When I first strapped it on I got a sense of what a gladiator must have felt like gearing up for battle, although getting plated with high-impact plastic instead of metal is admittedly somewhat different. Anyway, after racking up about a hundred dollars in rental fees, we rode our bikes to the lift entrance, with Brian wasting no time in getting the feel for his new set of wheels by riding it down the multiple steps of the building where the rental center was located.

While I could sense a lot of excitement building up as we rode the lift to the top of the mountain, the first run down on the main blue square trail ended up being somewhat tentative. Intellectually I knew the downhill bike would handle boulders and drops far better than my Enduro Pro could, but experientially I had no idea what that meant. It became a matter of taking small risks with obstacles at first and then gradually moving to bigger ones before I could gain a good sense of confidence about the bike's performance capabilities.

By the third run things seemed to be dialing in. I now felt confident enough to roll over a large boulder which I had steered around on the first two runs. I was surprised at how easy that maneuver was, and it made me want to take on more obstacles that were unthinkable for me to attempt with my regular bike. The more I tried the more impressed I became with just how versatile a heavy-duty suspension bike could be on challenging terrain.

There were still some tough spots, like the banked wooden track that allowed for a fast and tight turn in a dense section of trees. This one constantly tested me over and over as I sought to find the right amount of speed necessary to generate the centrifugal force that kept me turning on the track instead of flying off the top or falling over onto my side. Just out of that wooden turn, though, was my favorite section of the downhill course: a series of three trapezoid-shaped mounds underneath the chairlift, which Brian referred to as tables. Rolling over them reminded me of an undulating road that beckoned you to accelerate so you got a feeling of lift when you rolled over a hump and dipped down on the other side. It was a fun feeling, and each time I approached the tables I tried to take them a little bit faster, delighting in the up-and-down whipping effect I felt when I went over them.

On the fifth run, we felt confident enough to try a black diamond trail. It was hard, but not undoable, although it lacked the thrilling flow we'd managed to work up to on the intermediate runs. Along the way we saw a sign pointing to a double-black diamond trail, and on the chairlift heading back up the mountain for run number six, Brian lobbied hard to convince us to give it a try. Carl and I agreed, with some reluctance, but my prevailing sentiment was, *Why not? I can always bail out if I can't make it.*

The descent began with Carl and I pulling ahead of Brian, since he had to stop and buckle his helmet, which he'd forgotten to do before starting the run. Carl and I veered left at the double-black diamond sign and rolled along the trail for about ten to fifteen yards, then put the death grip to our brake handles. We skidded to a halt on top of a cliff, then turned to look at one another, waiting to see who would say it first.

"Forget this!" Carl said, speaking for both of us.

I validated his assertion with a loud "Amen!"

We turned our bikes around and made our way back to the turnoff, where Brian caught up with us.

"No way we're doing this," I said. "It's a cliff."

"Maybe some dirt you can catch in between the rocks, but I'm not going to try it." Carl added.

"More rocks than dirt—and steep!" I elaborated. "I'm not doing it either."

But Brian was undeterred. "Let me look," he said, and he pushed his bike around us and went on.

We waited for him there at the double-black diamond trail entrance, expecting him to return any moment, but to our surprise we heard his excited voice ringing through the trees, saying, "I can do this!"

With remarkable synchrony, Carl and I turned, looked at one another and pushed our eyebrows up toward the tops of our foreheads. "Are you sure?" we shouted back in unison.

"Oh, yeah," Brian answered. There was no need to shout back a second time to question his resolve, since the certainty was plainly evident in his voice.

"Wait until we get to the bottom so we can watch you!" I yelled.

Carl and I scrambled our bikes down the single black diamond section until we got to the location where the double-black diamond trail merged back into it. We then made our way through the woods, ending up on the hill off to the side of the cliff. From there we had a good view of Brian, who was poised on top.

Brian straddled his bike and looked down the cliff with unbroken concentration. It was impossible to know if he was thinking through how to navigate down the cliff face or simply trying to wrestle away any doubts or fears he had about taking the first drop over the edge. He rocked his bike back and forth between his legs as if it were a clock pendulum counting out some internal beat, perhaps a countdown before takeoff.

After a minute or so he settled back on his seat and propelled himself over the ledge. He wasn't airborne long before his wheels touched down onto a narrow line between two granite outcroppings, creating a flurry of dirt and pebbles that cascaded down the steep cliff face. He skidded for half a second then lashed around a stony protuberance before pointing his front wheel toward a downward-sloping section of rock with a flat surface. The instant he landed on it he brought his bike to a halt and angled the front wheel slightly to form a track stand. He kept a vise-like grip on his brake levers and alternated pressure between his right and left pedals to help him keep his balance.

"Good job!!" Carl shouted in encouragement.

"Way to go, Brian!" I added, amazed at just how little side-to-side wobbling he exhibited as he worked to maintain equilibrium on his perch atop the small rock.

Brian had landed his bike on the rock in such a way that it faced the hillside where Carl and I were witnessing the unfolding spectacle. I could see the intense concentration on Brian's face as he thought through his next move. With his feet still pressed tightly against his pedals, he bunny-hopped his bike several times, and with each up-

and-down motion he managed to incrementally rotate the bike back toward the downhill position.

Now set in the direction he wanted to go, Brian strained as he pushed against his left pedal to launch the bike over a vertical, washed-out chasm of dirt and stones and land on a large, horizontal obelisk further down the cliff face. There he had more room to rotate his bike with bunny-hops so he could continue the route down the cliff along his chosen path of descent. He pedaled off the obelisk and lunged through the air, clearing a large, round boulder and landing on the last steep section of dirt. At that point he loosened his grip on his brakes and hurtled down the rest of the cliff face before leveling out at the bottom.

Carl and I started jumping up and down and yelling wordless cries of astonishment. My shouts also contained a strain of relief, a release from the unspoken angst I felt from thinking that Brian might mess up on the way down and cause serious injury to himself. One misstep on that cliff would have resulted in a terrible amount of bodily harm. While I was excited he had conquered the challenge, the moment ushered in a turning point in my regard for him. From then on I harbored a secret fear that someday Brian was going to hurt himself badly—maybe even get himself killed—through an extreme exploit on one of his future outdoor adventures. Silently I thanked God that it didn't happen today, and prayed that it never would.

After the prayer I put my worry aside and left it in God's hands. It's not the kind of thing you want to keep thinking about anyway. Besides, we were still exulting over Brian's achievement, and so we quickly scurried back through the woods to meet him at the juncture of the two trails. We spent the next few minutes extolling Brian on how awesome his feat was, then resumed our praises after we completed the remainder of the downhill run and had reseated ourselves on the chairlift. Halfway up the mountain, Brian managed to get us to give it up by saying, "Enough, men. It was fun, but I don't think I'll do it again. The other trails are much more fun."

I was glad to hear that I wasn't missing out on anything special by not riding that double-black diamond run, but who was I kidding?

I knew I would never attempt something like that. Bringing the conversation back around to something a little more in line with my preferences, I said, "You know what I think is a fun section is those three tables underneath the chair lift."

"You know what you need to do…" Brian replied knowingly, "… is to clear the top of each table and land on the down ramp on the other side."

"Oh, yeah?" I asked, as if I had just learned I had been missing the whole point of table jumps all this time. I stared off into the blue sky above, seeing myself arcing over the tabletop and landing on the other side like a BMX pro, perhaps like Brian had been when he rode motorbikes. I thought about how cool that would look, and how that would allow me to make a mark on the day in some fashion. Maybe not as dramatic as Brian had done, but still admirable if I executed it correctly, especially if I did it on the first try. It was all I could think about until it came time to dismount from the chairlift and start riding.

Brian led the way as we started the seventh run down the mountain, followed by me, then Carl. By now we were handling the blue square trail like experts, flowing far faster than our very first ride down and now deliberately going out of our way to ride over obstacles. Before I knew it I was heading into the dense cluster of trees that encased the banked wooden platform. For the first time that day, I nailed the boards perfectly and emerged into the open area going pretty fast and feeling very confident. Sighting the tables ahead, I started rotating the crank with all I had, furiously pumping my legs in circles as if I were a little kid on a tricycle trying to escape a snarling dog chasing after me.

I hit the upward slope of the first table and shot up like a rocket, experiencing a thrust unlike anything felt during the first six runs of the day. The impulse was strong enough to force my firmly planted rear end off the seat and over the wheel, where the spinning tire hit between my butt cheeks like a rubber tipped buzz saw. It was such an alien sensation that I reflexively lifted up my rear end up to avoid what felt like a rotary proctological procedure. The bike responded like a seesaw and I was facing the down ramp as the front wheel landed on it. *Uh oh*, I said to myself, knowing where this was going to lead.

I'd cleared the tabletop, but the resulting compression and release of the front shock propelled me forward and free from the bike, and for the first time ever I got to experience what it would be like to fly prone through the air like my childhood hero, Superman. Unfortunately, I didn't glide to a nice two-point landing, arms akimbo at my side, ready to pounce on the next available villain like the caped superhero normally does. Instead, I did an arms-forward belly flop into the dirt just beside the second table. The last thing running through my mind before making contact with the ground was, *Did I remember to bring my insurance card with me?*

The impact knocked the breath out of me, but not so much that it would lead me to panic and jump up and try to get it back with desperate gasping noises. While still splayed in the dirt, I heard Carl's voice from behind me yelling, "Are you all right?"

I lifted my head and pushed myself up from what felt like a seabed of cinnamon. I stood and turned around, heart pumping like crazy, and grateful for all the plastic armor I was wearing that softened the landing into the dustbowl next to the tables. "Yeah, I'm okay," I answered.

Carl must have been holding it back for a few seconds, because once he heard those words, he burst out in some of the heartiest laughter I'd ever heard. He grabbed his stomach and doubled over as the guffaws gushed out like water from a fire hose. Actually, it made me feel kind of good that I could bring someone so much merriment, enough so that I momentarily forgot to look at the chairlift to see if I had to endure any embarrassment from any strangers that might have been passing by overhead at the same time and bearing witness to what just happened.

I hastened to the bathroom to wash the dust off my hands and face and, upon seeing my reflection in the mirror, I began to laugh as vigorously as Carl had. That part of my face that had been covered by my wrap-around sunglasses was completely dirt-free, while the rest of the face was dark brown, creating what looked like the markings of an off-color raccoon. It was so funny that I almost decided to hold off from washing up just so Brian could see how funny it looked.

We made one more run after that—with me taking the tables the way I knew I could handle them—then it was time to go. It had been an incredibly fun day under beautiful skies, and was everything that the day before wasn't. Later, as we chowed-down over burgers at a restaurant in Riggins, where we'd stopped for dinner on the way home, we recapped the highlights of the day like football sportscasters doing the big game wrap-up. Brian's double-black diamond run and my wipe out on the tables were the number one and number two plays of the day, respectively.

I'd coveted the kind of attention that Brian had received and I ended up getting it, but not in the way I thought I would. Maybe I could have avoided the crashing if I had just found contentment in the way my skills were progressing instead of trying to force something I wasn't ready for just to satisfy an unrighteous craving to share the spotlight with Brian. At least God gave me the grace to laugh it off instead of doubling-down in anger and frustration and attempting to try again to get it. What a great way to be reminded that building a life around misguided desires of possessing what others have will inevitably lead to the soul-crashing defeat of your spiritual walk.

"A THREE-STRANDED ROPE ISN'T EASILY SNAPPED"

August 3-4, 2014

How do you say goodbye to someone who's already gone? I don't know if the question crossed anybody else's mind that morning, but I think it was the reason for the silence in the room as we struggled with what to say. Seeing Brian hurt and broken, damaged beyond repair, I spoke first, acknowledging the secret fear I'd harbored since the time I'd watched him go down the cliff at the Tamarack Resort.

"Oh, Brian," I began, my voice soft and showing signs of cracking, "I was always afraid something like this would happen to you, but I never thought it would be like this. I'm going to miss you, brother. You've been a great friend and the best mountain-biking partner I could have ever had. You beat me to Heaven, but I'll see you there when it's my turn to go." As a gesture of tender affection I reached out and touched his cheek right below the ventilator tube. I began to weep as I choked out my final words: "Goodbye, my friend. I love you."

I backed away from the bedside so Jeremy could move closer to Brian to say his goodbyes. I heard the sadness and tenderness in his voice, but I was too overcome with sorrow to capture the words that he actually said. When he was finished, he moved over to me and we embraced each other, then Doug and Aaron moved in and wrapped their arms around us. Then an amazing thing happened. I was just moments away from collapsing with grief when that spontaneous bond of humanity infused me with a restoring surge of strength. As I felt myself lifted up, a Bible verse came to me, and for the first time, I viscerally understood exactly what it meant. It was Ecclesiastes 4:12: "By yourself you're unprotected. With a friend you can face the worst. Can you round up a third? A three-stranded rope isn't easily snapped" (MSG).

I left Brian's room down but not defeated. I thanked Doug for being there before he left to spend the rest of Sunday afternoon with his family, then I went to find Debbie. We hung around the hospital for a little while longer then, around mid-afternoon, exhaustion started to overwhelm us, so we drove home to catch a nap. Right before I lay down, I sent my three children a group text to let them know I was in mourning for my friend, and asked them to remember Brian's family in their prayers.

Debbie and I returned to the hospital at around five that afternoon, and by then everyone had moved up to the eleventh floor, where Ashley was recuperating. As we stepped out of the elevator we saw some folks seated in a small alcove near a window, so we joined them and inquired if they knew how things were going with Dena and the girls. As if on cue, Alicia appeared around the corner and Debbie beckoned her over and took her into her arms.

"How are you doing, Alicia?" she asked, her tender voice full of love and compassion.

"I'm a little sore right here," Alicia answered, pointing to an area across her chest. "That's where the seatbelt stopped me."

"Oh, Alicia, I'm so glad you were wearing your seatbelt," Debbie said as she hugged her.

"Five minutes before the accident happened I saw that I wasn't wearing it," Alicia confessed, "so I put it on."

Debbie and I glanced at each other, silently acknowledging how different a post-accident encounter with Alicia would have been had she not done that.

"Your guardian angel was watching over you," I explained, my voice expressing my deeply felt sincerity in that belief.

"Will you take us to your mommy's room?" Debbie asked.

Alicia nodded and led us to the room next to where Ashley was recuperating. There we saw Dena settled in along with her family members and some friends, among them Aaron Middleton. After greeting everyone I asked Dena how Ashley was doing.

"Fairly well," she responded. "The doctor said she is going to need a back brace, but she should heal up completely."

"That's encouraging," I said.

We chatted a bit more about how the injury might affect Ashley's plans to start college next month, then Dena said to me, "Can I ask a favor of you?"

"Sure. What is it?" I replied, eager to help in any way I could.

"Will you speak at Brian's memorial service?"

"Of course," I assured her, sensing inside that God was calling me to do this but using Dena as the vehicle for making His purpose known. "When is the service?"

"This Saturday."

Just then Aaron jumped in with a follow-up question. "Did Brian ever tell you about his 'I Am Second' testimony?"

"He told me about the concept. You dress up in black and sit in a spotlight on a white chair and film your testimony. He said the youth group at your church had started doing it."

Aaron nodded. "He's been working on it since spring but we decided it would be better for him to wait to deliver it to the youth group during the first part of the fall program, when everyone was back from summer vacation," he explained. "Do you know where he might have kept it?"

"Probably on his laptop from work. Do you know where that is?"

"It was in his backpack," Dena said. "He had it with him in the van."

"Is there any way you can get it to me?"

"I'll see what I can do," Aaron said.

I didn't want to discourage Aaron, but I knew it was going to take a specialist to get into Brian's laptop, since all laptops from our work were encrypted. Yet, deep down, I was intrigued with the challenge of finding the missing manuscript, and had faith that somehow God would provide a way for us to retrieve it.

Debbie and I left shortly after that and as soon as I got home I checked my text messages. Both of my daughters had texted me back to express their sympathy and condolences about Brian's death, but to my surprise I still had not heard back from my son, Zack. I figured I must have selected his work phone number instead of his mobile when I sent the group message, so I resent the original text to him.

Zack replied five minutes later saying he'd heard about what had happened earlier that morning from his mom. Then he offered to take some time off that week to come be with us. I recounted some of the events that had happened that day, and he talked about how he remembered Brian being a really nice and gracious person, and how much fun he had playing flag football with him during Turkey Bowl 2006, an annual Thanksgiving day event that the men and youth of the Nazarene Church held at the Clarkston High School football field.

"I read that 'Seven Great Men' book I received at Christmas," he continued texting, "…and it really helped me understand a lot of things about being a great person that touches people's lives. I bet there's a lot in Brian's life that we can learn from and would be able to reflect on."

"Yes, there is," I wrote back. "I have written down a lot about him in my unfinished book, 'Lessons from the Trail.'" It was a book I'd been working off and on for about six years, and only Brian and Zack knew about it.

"Yeah, I was thinking a lot about that book," Zack responded. "I bet there's a lot of lessons that were taught through him. I think it would be a great honor to him to write that, almost in a way to share his legacy with others."

I thought about it for about ten minutes before I texted back, "Yeah, that's what I've been thinking," but I'm sure that didn't accurately communicate just how recent that thinking was.

"Keep me posted on the plans for the week. I'm going to try to get back for the funeral."

"Will do," I replied before signing off for the night and getting some much-needed sleep.

Monday morning came and along with it the normal weekday routine. I went to work at the usual time, but sensed a strange disconnectedness with everyone I was accustomed to working with. I felt like a foreigner in a country where no one understood me and, a couple of times, I shut the door to my office, planted my face against the wall and wept uncontrollably.

A few work associates knew about my friendship with Brian and perhaps they understood my doleful appearance, but the majority of folks did not. Remembrances of yesterday's long day at the hospital and the ever-growing realization that Brian was no longer going to be a part of any of our lives distracted me from doing the basic duties at the office. Seeing how helpless I was with my normal routine, I started struggling over how I was going to ever find the time and energy to put together the message I'd committed to give at Brian's memorial service. I felt like I was trying really hard to get somewhere but was getting nowhere, just like that night in January, some seven and a half years earlier, on a remote snowfield in southeastern Washington.

LOST

Nestled in the southeast corner of Washington State is Fields Spring State Park, named after Ben Fields, a homesteader who built a water collection system for a spring that was there. The park sits on the rim of the Grande Ronde Canyon and the spring is still actively utilized, providing deliciously cool and sweet-tasting water that I've used to fill the blue bladder of my CamelBak for more rides there than I can count. In the center of the park is a prominent geographical feature called Puffer Butte. This feature was also named after a homesteader, but I like to imagine it got its name on account of all the huffing and puffing one does to pedal to the top of it. It's worth the effort, though, as the reward is some quick and exciting singletrack descents. Encircling Puffer Butte are mostly easy trails with spectacular views of the canyon and distant mountains in Idaho and Oregon.

In winter all these pathways get transformed into cross-country skiing trails, and every winter Brian would start lobbying me to take up backcountry skiing, a sport he and Jeremy pursued with the same passion that Brian and I reserved for mountain biking. I was reluctant to take Brian up on his invitation. For one thing, I'm not a good downhill skier, and really not that good of a cross-country skier, unless it's across flat terrain. Brian and Jeremy favored frolicking on steep mountains, often in wilderness areas, a big jump for my meager skiing skills. Nevertheless, the lure of outdoor adventures in remote, snow-blanketed terrains along with Brian's stories of his experiences with Jeremy made me want to give it a try.

Since I was a novice at the sport, I felt it would be wise to build up my capabilities for doing backcountry skiing before ever heading out with Brian and Jeremy. Being familiar with the topography of Fields Spring, I figured that was a good place to start, especially since I'd done some cross-country skiing there before. So, I started talking up the idea of doing a Saturday night run around Puffer Butte with several folks, and before long two acquaintances had responded favorably to my plans: Bob Dice and Justin Moss.

Bob was my next-door neighbor, the one who had recommended the Twenty Mile trail that we rode the same weekend Brian rode down the cliff at the Tamarack Resort. Bob was also the manager of the Blue Mountain Region for the Washington State Fish and Wildlife. Besides being a good neighbor, Bob was also a mountain biker as well as a valuable friend to the mountain-biking community in the Lewiston-Clarkston Valley. Every spring he would help us get trail maintenance equipment up into the Asotin Creek Trail, a popular local riding destination. We'd trim branches and chainsaw through fallen trees, as well as clear the rocks that had broken free from the stony crags above and tumbled down the side of the canyon. He'd ridden with Brian and me several times over the course of our friendship.

Justin was a high-tech do-it-yourselfer that could diagnose and fix just about anything wrong with a computer system. He was my co-worker in the information technology department at the pulp and paper mill in Lewiston and had just six months earlier convinced me to join him on the rocky and strenuous climb to the top of Sacajawea Peak in the Eagle Cap Wilderness Area, whose lofty mountains are visible from Fields Spring. Justin was no stranger to outdoor adventures, either. He once had a life-threatening encounter with a bear in his camping tent, which he resolved with a firearm that he prudently kept with him whenever he was in remote backcountry.

I met Bob in the parking lot of the local high school, where I had just finished watching my daughter Emily play a game of basketball. I transferred my gear from the Xterra to the bed of his pickup truck and we took off. Fat flakes of snow floated past the headlights as we slowly made our way up the slick, serpentine turns of Washington State Highway 129 as it climbed out of the Snake River Canyon. The road flattened out once we reached the prairie on top, and the treacherous driving conditions abated. Near Rattlesnake Summit, about a mile from the park entrance, we entered a thick fog bank that seemed to filter out the larger snowflakes, allowing only light flecks to land on the windshield. Shortly after that we pulled into the main parking lot of Fields Spring, where we spotted a truck idling with its parking lights on.

"There's Justin," I said.

Bob pulled up alongside and killed the motor. I hopped out and went over to greet Justin. "Been here long?" I asked.

"About a half hour," he replied.

"Sorry," I said, feeling bad that we'd made him wait so long. "The road was pretty slippery on the way up the grade and then we ran into some fog," I offered as an excuse.

Bob stepped forward to introduce himself, and the three of us bantered about some friendly chatter before getting down to the purpose of our late-night rendezvous. "Which trails were you thinking about doing?" Justin asked.

I already had that figured out. "Let's just take the old farm road that goes around Puffer Butte. We can do it clockwise. That way we'd get to ski the steepest part in the downhill direction."

Bob and Justin nodded, both apparently willing to follow my lead for the evening.

"The road fades out at a large clearing right before you get to the canyon rim," I continued, "but I know where to turn to get back on it."

"If the fog lifts maybe we can ski over to the rim and take a look in the canyon." Bob suggested. "It might be pretty cool to see it at night."

"Sounds good," I said. "Let's do it."

We changed into our cross-country ski boots, locked into the long and slender runners and took off. First we skied past the park's main lodge and then slipped onto a groomed trail at the gate that kept out unauthorized vehicles. Soon we reached the first of two livestock gates that enclose a free-range area on the loop around Puffer Butte. As we worked the gate open so we could ski through, I noticed in the LED beam of my headlamp that the snow had transformed into rain, which meant the ambient temperature had shifted above the freezing point sometime after we'd left the parking lot.

All three of us were bummed out when we saw that the trail on the other side of the gate was no longer groomed. With the conditions turning somewhat soggy, it didn't take long for large clumps of snow to build up on our skis. Any attempt to glide felt like grating across asphalt on two-by-fours. The elevation change I'd mentioned we'd get to do in the downhill direction was a total bust, as the pull of gravity was useless against the adhesiveness of the wet and lumpy snow. Even on the steepest part of the descent it took a lot of work, as evidenced by our need to stop and unzip various layers of clothing to release the body heat that was building up from all the exertion it took to move forward.

When we'd made it to the bottom of the hill, we huddled up. "Still want to ski over to the rim?" I asked.

"No, it's not worth it now," Bob answered. "It's still too foggy to see much of anything and with this snow it's probably not worth the effort to ski there."

Justin agreed. "Let's skip it and head on around Puffer Butte."

"Okay. After we reach the clearing we'll need to start looking for the path to get us back on the farm road," I informed them.

Bob and Justin trusted me to continue leading so I pushed onward until the snow covered cut in the terrain dissipated, indicating we'd reached the area where the farm road faded out. I started looking ahead for the right turn that I'd made so many times before on my mountain bike, but the poor visibility interfered with my ability to read the lay of the land, and the light from my headlamp wasn't bright enough to illuminate the familiar landmarks that readily indicated where I needed to go. Silently, I coached myself along: *Any moment now. Any moment now.*

As I kept looking for something familiar that would signal it was time to turn, I started getting anxious that I hadn't yet seen anything. Fueling that anxiety was the vain need to avoid hesitation so that I wouldn't appear like I didn't know what I was doing in front of my friends and cause them to lose confidence in me. *Any moment now,* I repeated silently, feeling a strong impulse to make a move. Then I saw a break between a patch of hardwood trees. *There,* I told myself hopefully. *That's got to be it!*

"Here we go," I shouted. "Just up this hill a little ways then we hit the farm road."

My first impression heading up the slope was that the hill seemed steeper than usual, but I attributed that to the difference in perspective between skiing up versus biking up. Still, it was taking more effort than I thought to reach the broad cut in the landscape that signaled we had returned to the farm road. It wasn't long before the strain from climbing generated so much more body heat that I had to take my jacket completely off and tie it around my waist.

"Darn! We should be seeing that road now," I said with enough irritation in my voice to suggest I was getting angry at the road for not doing what it was supposed to do.

We trudged on, the ground sloping off a little but still climbing upward, until Justin hollered, "Hold up for a moment. Something's wrong with one of my skis."

Bob and I made our way back and spotted our headlamps onto Justin as he sat there on the snow, trying to remove the ski so he could get a better look at it. "I've had this happen before," he admitted as he fiddled with his binding.

"Can you fix it?" I asked.

"Oh, yeah, I fixed it the last time it happened."

"Tell you what, then. Bob and I will keep going until we hit the farm road. We'll wait for you there. It's not far and you can follow our tracks." I had chosen my words carefully to make it sound reassuring that we were on the right track, but deep inside I was bothered that I hadn't found the road and beginning to fret that something had gone wrong. Perhaps more for my benefit than Bob or Justin's, I added, "We should be there now anyway."

Justin started working on his binding as Bob and I resumed climbing. Soon we entered a glade of evergreens, another unfamiliar landmark that should have made me stop and think. Well, in a sense it did make me do one of those action steps, as I skied too close to one of the trees and in an instant found myself up to my waist in quicksand-like snow. The more I struggled to get out, the more I sank in.

"Hey, Bob! I'm stuck in a tree well," I hollered in frustration.

"Are you all right?"

"Yeah. Why don't you keep going until you reach the road? I'll wait here until Justin catches up and then we'll meet you there."

"You sure?"

"Yeah. We should be there by now anyway," I answered, repeating the hollow refrain from earlier.

As Bob took off, I kept up the struggle to free myself from the snow well, but to no avail. In a few moments I was too exhausted to move anymore, so I simply gave up the fight and just hovered there in the powdery suspension, stuck chest deep in the unforgiving whiteness. I believe that was a blessing now, as the only thing I could do in that motionless state was to think. One by one the misguided thoughts that had brought me to this state of helplessness began to recede and the one idea that I had been suppressing ever since I made the right turn that led the three of us up that small hill came to the forefront of my mind: We'd made a wrong turn and now we were lost.

Our situation reminded me of what was in the news about a month and a half earlier, when three expert climbers had attempted to scale the north face of Mt. Hood and had gotten *fatally* lost. I began to wonder if we were going to repeat that story. Of course, the conditions at Fields Spring were nowhere near as severe as what those climbers faced on Mt. Hood, but still, overnight in the woods, raining, wet snow all around, tired, no food, no water…it didn't seem to lead to a good outcome. I shuddered then fell back into the false but consoling self-talk: *But the road just has to be there. It HAS to!*

I shook my head, told myself to shut up, and looked at my watch. We'd been out skiing for an hour and a half now. If indeed we were lost, we could just follow our tracks out of the glade and back to where we started, even though I knew the return ascent up the steep hill would really test the limits of our endurance. Despite the tremendous challenge posed by backtracking our way out, I began to believe it was our only option.

Turning my head around, I hollered through the darkness and fog, "Hold up, Justin! We may have a change of plans."

"I haven't moved yet," Justin yelled back. "I'm still trying to fix the binding."

"Bob is on a scouting expedition to find the farm road," I shouted back. Then, turning my head forward, I yelled, "Bob! Have you found the road yet?"

"Not yet," came the answer from the woods up above.

I passed the next couple of minutes removing my skis and maneuvering them on top of the snow surface, reasoning that would make it easier for me to escape the white pit I was in. Then I hollered again, "Bob! Have you found it yet?"

"Not yet," he repeated.

I started experimenting with using my skis as stakes in the snow in front of me to help pull me out. It was working, and after a few minutes of making progress, I paused to holler out at Bob a third time. "Have you found it yet?"

Like the first two times, he yelled back, "Not yet," but this time his words seemed far away. Really far away.

Oh my gosh, I thought, *He's skied halfway up to the top of Puffer Butte!*

"That's it! We've made a wrong turn!" I finally admitted, shouting as loud as I could as if to confess my error to all of creation. "We have to go back. Bob, come on back down. We're going to backtrack to get out of here. Justin, stay where you are. We're coming back."

"I still haven't gone anywhere," Justin responded, his voice cracking with exasperation.

By the time Bob made it back to the glade I had managed to extract myself completely from the snow well. I lumbered away from the trees with knee-deep steps before putting my skis back on, and Bob and I skied back to where Justin was waiting. His binding was broken worse than he had originally thought, and unlike his ability to fix anything that was wrong with computers and their associated technology, there was no fixing this. Feeling guilty for getting them into this predicament with my bad navigation skills, I offered Justin the use of my skis, but he adamantly declined. I worried about how he was going to get back up the steep hill without them, but then again, it wasn't going to be that easy with them.

We got out of the wooded area and started backtracking toward the edge of the clearing. This approach provided a different orientation toward the landscape, and just as we reached the spot where we'd made the wrong right turn, I caught a glimpse of groomed track toward the end of the beam of my headlamp. I scooted in that direction without saying a word to either Bob or Justin. Then I saw it: the right turn we should have made an hour ago. Had we just skied a few more yards past where we turned the first time, we would have spotted it.

"Hey, Bob, Justin! This way! This is the way to the road. I'm positive. Trust me!"

To this day I don't know how they could trust my directional instincts again after I had acted so absolutely certain about where the trail picked up the first time, only to commit an extraordinary blunder that wasted our time and energy. Yet Bob and Justin slowly trekked over to where I was now standing and surveyed the area. I suppose it wasn't my word that convinced them, but the evidence of seeing a groomed trail again. At that point it was easy to conclude logically that it was the way we needed to go. As we plodded forward through the darkness, I kept telegraphing what to expect next, thinking I needed to restore what I thought was their lost confidence in me. Still, no matter how much knowledge I could demonstrate about the trail it wasn't enough to overcome the inferiority I felt for that one deficiency that caused such a mess of things.

Eventually, we made it back to the parking lot. We skied over to our rigs (the Inland Northwest vernacular for pickups, SUVs, and other heavy-duty vehicles) and warily removed our ski equipment. Bob and Justin seemed gracious about the whole affair—no anger or bitterness, just a solid determination to pack up the gear and go home. It was past midnight, and way past the times we had pledged to our spouses we would return, so we dispensed without any further chitchat and said goodnight to one another.

Debbie must have been sleeping lightly when I came home, because the first thing I heard coming from the bedroom was her voice saying, "You're late. What happened?"

"We got turned around and couldn't find the trail for a while," I responded, trying to impart a non-dramatic, matter-of-fact tone to minimize any further exploration of the topic.

Standing bedside, I stripped off my wet clothes down to the thermal layer then headed toward the dining room, where I poured myself a glass of brandy and eased myself down onto one of the wooden chairs that surrounded the table. I sat there in silence, sipping at my glass while the aches slowly faded, allowing the amber liquid to soothe my body and warm my soul as I thought about what I had just been through. Missing that turn had been an unwitting mistake, and right away there had been a plethora of signs that we were off course: the steepness of the hill, the length of time it took to get there and even the glade of trees were all things that I knew we shouldn't have encountered on the way to the farm road, but still I kept believing we were going to reach it at any moment. How could I have ignored the obvious?

I realized then that there's a certain psychology that starts to come into play when you get lost in the outdoors. First, it's hard to admit that you've gotten off track, even when the warning signs around you suggest that you have. Instead of paying attention to those signs and trying to figure out what they mean, you begin to look for ways to justify the incongruence and rationalize why it's not important; in some cases, you outright ignore those signs. Thus you keep telling yourself that you just need to go a little more this way and everything will be all right. *I'll be there. I'll reach my goal.* And on and on you go, deeper and deeper, until you get too far into the wrong way and suddenly it's not all right and you've gone past the point of returning back to where the right path was.

At least tonight we didn't get to that point, I thought to myself as I savored the last few sips of brandy. I couldn't help but wonder if that's what happened to the Mt. Hood climbers: they made a wrong decision but kept going, thinking they were going to be all right, until they realized they'd gotten themselves into a hopeless situation. As I made my way to bed, I shivered to think about how quickly an adventure can turn into a tragedy all on account of one small mistake left unchecked.

Life itself is full of episodes of getting lost at Fields Spring. We commit an error in moral judgment—a sin—and when the consequences of our wrongdoing start manifesting themselves, we figure out ways to ignore them so we can continue along our wayward path. We try really hard to get somewhere when in fact, we get nowhere.

Then as things start getting really bad we justify the mess we've gotten ourselves into with grand notions that rationalize why things are really okay, fooling ourselves temporarily so we can trudge onward to our undoing. I believe the root of this behavior is a pride that won't let us admit we've made a mistake. Maybe that's one reason why it's said that pride is the worst of all sins. It blinds you to what's really going, thereby preventing you from repenting and getting your life back on track. At Fields Spring, my stubbornness in continuing on down the wrong path was born out of my egotistical desire to avoid looking bad in front of Bob and Justin. Ironically, that attitude only led to an even worse loss of face.

Given that sanctification is a lifelong process, we can expect to continue to get lost in this world. Maybe we come to our senses before it's too late and admit we've made an error, or maybe our world comes crashing down around us and we never figure it out, or maybe the crash brings us to our knees before God, whose radiance and truth expose the self-duplicity of our ways and lead us to repentance. When we do come to our senses, we have a loving father in Heaven who is ready to embrace us the same way the father embraced his prodigal son when he returned from his wayward journey (see Luke 15: 11-32). Jesus died for our sins so we wouldn't have to stay lost, if we will only admit it. Fields Spring taught me to not waste time in forsaking my pride and admitting the error of my ways so I can be restored onto the right paths that God has in store for me.

A GREATER PURPOSE

August 4, 2014

When work ended that Monday afternoon, I felt physically and emotionally drained. My normal after work routine called for stopping at the gym on the way home and doing some powerlifting, but today it seemed pointless to believe I could summon the drive needed to do train at the level of intensity that that type of workout required. Instead, I went straight to the hospital where I met Dena's brother who was also named Brian, but family members called him Birdsell (his surname) to avoid confusion.

"Your wife is Debbie, right?" Birdsell inquired.

"Yes," I acknowledged.

"She was up here earlier and I gave her Brian's laptop to give to you."

"Oh, did Aaron Middleton say something to you about seeing if I could find Brian's 'I Am Second' testimony on it?" I asked.

"No. I just know you both work for the same company and that you could see that their property got returned to them," Birdsell explained.

"Thanks. I'll make sure it gets back."

After a short conversation about the types of jobs we held, Birdsell said, "You know they're still keeping Brian on life support."

"No, I didn't," I admitted, somewhat puzzled. "I thought he was declared to be brain-dead."

"Yeah, but they need to keep his organs alive until they're ready to be donated."

I had never thought about it before, but it suddenly made sense. Contacting recipients, getting them scheduled for surgery, and arranging the logistics to transport the organs from Spokane to wherever just doesn't happen instantly. "Do you know when they will start harvesting the organs?" I asked.

"Tuesday night. There's going to be a blessing for a lot of people, that's for sure."

"For sure," I echoed. Knowing how healthy Brian had been when he was alive, those recipients were going to be very fortunate indeed.

"Do you know a reputable crematorium service that I could contact for handling Brian's remains," Birdsell asked.

"I know someone who would know." I replied. "Hold on while I find out."

I pulled out my phone and started texting Doug Weinrich, asking if he would get up with our church's senior pastor and ask for a recommendation. As I typed out the message, a realization slowly dawned on me. I was a key contact for Dena and her family for answering questions and fulfilling requests that involved having a working knowledge of Spokane. For the first time I discerned a greater purpose as to why I had been transferred to Spokane seven years ago. I froze momentarily, awestruck at God's sovereignty over all the decisions that others and I had made which affected my life's trajectory, only to have me arrive at a place and time where I could be of service to his people in their hour of need.

"What's wrong?" Birdsell asked.

"Nothing," I responded, snapping out of it. "I'm just honored I can be of service."

On the way home from the hospital that evening I got a call from Bob Dice, still my friend even after the Fields Spring fiasco, and I returned his call when I got home. He'd heard what had happened to Brian and just wanted to talk about it and see how I was doing. Then he told me he was going to be in Spokane tomorrow and asked if we could meet up for lunch. I said, "Sure," and he said he would call me around eleven thirty to coordinate the exact time and place.

As soon as I got home, Debbie told me she had left the backpack that Birdsell had given her in the back of her car. I retrieved it and then went into dining room and began emptying its contents. Naturally, the first thing I pulled out was the laptop, followed by some other of Brian's personal effects. The laptop had been cracked open in one corner, and I worried about the condition of the hard drive given the kind of blow it must have taken to damage it like that. Well, that was something for the experts to figure out, so I put it next to my briefcase so I could remember to take it with me into work the next day.

"LET'S PRAY"

August 5, 2014

Tuesday morning I got up and prayed then headed off to work again. My day was booked with six hours' worth of meetings, and feeling like a zombie during the first one pretty much set the expectation for how the rest would proceed. Fortunately, that first meeting ended early, so I took Brian's laptop to Jared Pauletto, a technical analyst in the information technology department where I worked and a Christian brother whom I could trust. Jared and I had been on a couple of mountain bike rides at Riverside State Park just west of Spokane. He knew the trail system there as well as he knew the sectors of a laptop hard drive, so if anybody could recover the document—assuming it was on the hard drive—it would be him. I told him to look for a Word file named either "I Am Second" or "Testimony," and left it with him as I headed for the next meeting.

During the next hour Doug got back to me with the recommendation for the crematorium, which I relayed to Birdsell. Not too long after that Birdsell called me, and I excused myself from the meeting to talk. He said he'd worked out the arrangements with the crematorium already and then asked if I could get up with our benefits department to get some insurance information for Dena. I only had the lunch hour to get that done, so I contacted Bob and asked if he could meet me for coffee after work instead, and he was good to go with the change in plans.

The rest of the day was like speeding and sleepwalking at the same time, and everything remained a blur. I left work at four thirty so I could rendezvous with Bob at a coffee shop just one block from where I worked. I told Bob all that had happened since Saturday night, and then we reminisced about all the times we'd ridden together with Brian.

"Do you remember the first time I went riding with you and Brian?" he asked.

I wasn't sure, since we'd been on lots of rides together. "Was that on Moscow Mountain?"

"Yeah. We'd just gotten all of our gear on and mounted our bikes. I'm getting ready to take off and Brian says, 'Let's pray.'" Bob paused and began chuckling. "And I'm thinking, 'Where is this guy taking me? This is just a bike ride. Is there a chance I'm not going to survive it?'"

"Huh," I grunted, momentarily drifting off to another time. "I know what you mean. I was once on a ride with Brian where I thought the same thing."

FAITH

I grew up far from the Pacific Northwest in a small town called Pembroke, nestled among the foothills of Southwest Virginia between the Appalachian Plateau and the Blue Ridge Mountains. Place names seemed to have a divine ring about them in that part of the country. The next little burg east of Pembroke is the community of Hoges Chapel, where—appropriately—I attended a little country church as a lad. There is a mountain in the town where I went to high school called Angel's Rest. Further east is the city of Christiansburg, part-time residence of such pioneer explorers as Davy Crocket and Daniel Boone.

Not so with Clarkston, my first home in the Pacific Northwest. For instance, travelers crossing over from Idaho are greeted with a sign proclaiming, "Welcome to Clarkston, Gateway to Hells Canyon." Clarkston is named after William Clark of Lewis and Clark fame, who camped in the area on their journey to and from the Pacific Ocean, and it sits on a bend of the Snake (*think serpent*) River. Then there's one of Washington's premier epic mountain bike rides located near Wenatchee: Devil's Gulch. At the time it held the claim of being the longest singletrack in the state.

Once Brian and I found out about Devil's Gulch, we knew we just had to go. After over a year of trying to coordinate a time when we could make it, we finally landed on the first Saturday in November of 2008. My guess was that early November was probably the latest time of the year anyone would attempt to ride Devil's Gulch, given the increased likelihood of encountering snowfall at the higher elevations of the trail. Anyway, it felt good that even though we now lived a hundred miles apart, we could still find a way to make special road trips for epic rides.

The alarm went off at 4:30 a.m. and I was out the door within the next half hour, cradling a large thermos of hot coffee between my legs as I drove away from my new home in Spokane, which I'd only lived in for three months. I felt rested and ready to let the caffeine shake the scales from my eyes. Local traffic was spotty at best, and all lights were green as I made my way to I-90. After about an hour travelling through the dark I saw the exit sign for the little farm community of Sprague. I pulled out my phone and called Brian to ask where he was. He said he was just now getting on the freeway. Ahead, I saw a car merging from the on-ramp.

"Did you just go through Sprague?" I asked.

"Yes."

I accelerated so I could pull up closer behind the car in front of me and I made out the silhouette of a bike on top. "I'm right behind you," I said, pleased that our plans on when to leave and where we might rendezvous had worked out so perfectly.

The next exit was a rest stop and Brian suggested we pull off there to take a bathroom break. From there, Brian followed me west on I-90 to Exit 151, then north to Quincy before heading west on Highway 28 to Wenatchee, where we watched the first glints of daylight illuminate the majestic cliffs of the Columbia Plateau. We crossed the Columbia River at Wenatchee, then followed the shallow autumn waters of the Wenatchee River to the small town of Cashmere, with its odd-looking roofs covering the sidewalks and cross walks in the historic downtown section. After a little trial and error, I found the turn onto Mission Creek Road, named after the creek that drained Devil's Gulch, and finally arrived at the trailhead.

Brian pulled his van next to my Xterra and we wasted no time in getting geared up for the ride. After looking over the map one more time, we decided to just start riding up the forest service road, thinking that would be the quickest way to get to the top of Devil's Gulch. From there we would ride down the trail, load the bikes up on the Xterra, drive back to the top and downhill it again, finishing with a final shuttle ride back to the top in Brian's van to retrieve the Xterra. It was an ambitious plan, very much reflective of our appetite for riding.

After we prayed, I activated my GPS and waited for it to pick up enough satellites to triangulate our position. I also brought along a photocopy of an area map from a mountain-biking trail guidebook and a printout from an online guide to getting to the upper trailhead, which featured directions that included mile markers correlated with major turns and landmarks. The GPS would measure our progress up the mountain and help us locate those navigational points.

We began the long crank up the rugged forest service road, past giant granite outcroppings that bulged out of the mountainside like mighty biceps, past glowing tamaracks that seemed to reflect a hidden illumination source as they blazed against the withering landscape. The sun had yet to break through the clouds that morning, and a heaviness hung in the air as if it were fully saturated with cool moisture. The forecast called for a 30 percent chance of rain, and we figured the odds were good that we would get through the day without getting any precipitation. Even when the first few drops started to fall, we dismissed it as just a slight shower that would soon pass.

I felt somewhat exerted after the first half hour of climbing, and so I lobbied Brian to take a break. The rain had picked up a little so we sought shelter under the trees as we chomped down on energy snacks. The fueling stop only took about five minutes, but it set the pattern for the rest of the ride up the mountain—crank for about thirty minutes, then refuel for five. The rain stayed light throughout the entire climb but was steady enough to dampen the outer layer of our clothes.

I kept a close watch of the GPS output throughout the climb and got good agreement between the mileage readings and what the directions said I should expect at those readings. But then we encountered a fork in the road at a mile-mark that wasn't listed on the directions, so I told Brian to hold up for a second while I got out the map.

"I don't see the fork on here," I concluded after several minutes of intense study.

"Let me see," said Brian.

I passed him the map. "We have a fifty-fifty chance of taking the right road," I stated.

Brian looked at the map for a few minutes then shrugged. "It looks like the main part of the road goes this way," he indicated with his arm stretched out toward the left.

"That's what I think," I replied, so we took off in that direction.

After less than five minutes of riding, we encountered a sign pointing out that we were entering the Beehive Reservoir Area.

"Wrong way," I announced as I hit the brakes. "I remember seeing this area on one of the online maps. It's in a direction away from the trailhead."

"Well, at least we didn't get too far," Brian said.

We turned around and headed back to the fork, taking the other road when we got there. We pedaled on for another five to ten minutes when I uttered, "Oh, crap."

"What?" Brian asked.

"I forgot to check the GPS when we got back to the fork. Now I don't know exactly how many miles off we are from the mile markers in the directions, meaning I don't have an accurate reading for when we reach the trailhead."

"It couldn't be more than a couple of miles," Brian reckoned.

I thought about it for a moment then said, "Based on the total miles alone, we would almost be there, so let's just keep a good lookout on the right hand side of the road from this point forward."

We resumed cranking up the mountain and it wasn't long before we passed a clearing on the right. It looked like one of those areas where loggers parked their road-building or tree-harvesting equipment in between cuttings. I'd seen places like that before on Moscow

Mountain, and indeed, parked at the edge of the clearing about fifty feet from the road was a vintage-looking grader. I didn't think much more about it, and Brian must not have either, as he pedaled on by the entrance to the clearing without wavering.

The road past the clearing began to get steeper and, feeling the power in my legs starting to flag, I slipped the chain into a lower gear. We'd climbed about 3,400 feet of elevation already and the fatigue from the effort was slowing my forward progress. The landscape off to the right was consistently devoid of any break in the brush and forest that would indicate the start of a trail. I was quickly running out of steam, but I kept cranking, believing we'd find the trailhead any moment. *We should be there by now,* I thought to myself.

Then it hit me: *Where have I said that before?* Then I remembered, and immediately yelled out to Brian, "All right, we've missed it. We need to turn around and go back to the intersection and start again."

"No," Brian objected. "Just a little bit more and I'm sure we'll find it."

"No, no, this isn't right," I insisted. "We've passed what would be a reasonable offset on the GPS based on the wrong turn. We've missed the trailhead and need to turn back and find it."

Brian was adamant. "No we haven't. It can't be far from here. We just need to keep going."

"I understand how you feel, Brian, but we're lost!" Then, clearing my throat and calming my voice, I asked, "Did I ever tell you the story about the night Bob Dice and Justin Moss and I went cross-country skiing around Fields Spring and I got us lost?"

"No."

"I was probably too embarrassed to talk about it, but let me tell you what happened."

As I relayed that fateful trip around Puffer Butte that night nearly two years ago, I could see the determination in Brian's face start to fade away. When I had finished, Brian had abandoned his resistance to heading back. We turned our bikes around and took off back down the stretch of mountain that we had just climbed.

Within moments we were gliding past the clearing. This time I paid extra scrutiny to the area, which led me to notice a detail that I had overlooked the first time: wooden beams embedded into a small mound of earth, which made it look like a place where you back up a trailer to unload horses. I remembered reading that equestrians were also users of the Devil's Gulch Trail, so I turned into the clearing to take a closer look.

Brian stopped and said, "I'll wait here," apparently skeptical that this was the spot where the trailhead started.

I dismounted my bike when I reached the earthen berm with the wooden beams, and after scrambling over it I saw a smooth ribbon of singletrack heading off into the woods.

"This is it! The trailhead!" I shouted jubilantly, so glad to have finally found it.

"But your directions didn't mention a clearing or a parking lot."

"I know, but they're probably old directions and it looks like this area was just recently built. That would explain why the road grader is here. Come and see!"

Brian wheeled over to look. A big, radiant grin lit up his face. "Yep! This is it! Let's go!"

His sudden burst of enthusiasm was contagious, but I was feeling awfully fatigued from all the climbing—and extra climbing, too. "Let's fuel up first," I pleaded, knowing that even though we had lots of miles of downhill ahead of us, we'd still need the energy to get through it.

We removed our CamelBaks and dug through the deep pockets, pulling out packets of assorted snacks to share with each other. I liked the high-tech nourishment—gels and gummies infused with electrolytes and caffeine-laced jellybeans—while Brian preferred the whole food approach: almonds, chocolate, beef jerky (which he once told me he liked to put between his gum and cheek and let it slowly dissolve while he rode) and pretzel nuggets filled with peanut butter. As we feasted we heard a sound from behind us. We turned and saw a short and somewhat squat-looking biker emerge from the trail, the pale white complexion of his face making it appear almost as if he was glowing.

"How goes it?" Brian shouted at him.

The man turned and saw us, and I waved, trying to appear friendly. He pulled his bike over by us and removed his helmet, revealing a thick head of white hair which matched the complexion of his face. "Nice day for mountain biking," he said.

It was hard to tell if he was being sincere or sarcastic with the statement, so I ventured a neutral response. "At least you won't get overheated riding on a day like today."

Brian picked up the conversation from there while I silently sized up our visitor. He had to be in his late sixties, I thought. Yet, it seemed admirable that someone his age would be out mountain biking alone, especially in rugged country like this.

"Would you like to try some of this homemade trail mix?" Brian asked as he extended the plastic bag of treats toward him.

"No thank you," he said politely. Then he reached into his trail sack and pulled out a tiny cylindrical case. He popped open the top and shook out three white capsules, the same color as his face and hair. "I take these to prevent muscle cramps," he revealed, popping the capsules into his mouth followed by a measured gulp of water from the tube emerging from his hydration pack.

"I've never heard of such a thing," I confessed, curious to learn more.

"I got a prescription for them," he replied. "Do you want to try them?"

The offer startled me, and there was silence between the three of us as I tried to process what was going on right then. First of all, I couldn't imagine going to a doctor solely for a prescription for medicine to prevent cramps while exercising. Then, I couldn't imagine someone offering a stranger a dose of his prescription medicine. But here's the funny thing: Something inside of me was telling me to say yes.

"No thank you," I blurted out, contrary to the conviction of my inner impulses. Right away I realized I was lying, but I was just trying to be polite, since it seemed to me that taking something like that from our elderly guest would be an imposition.

"Okay," he said with a tone of voice that suggested he was aware I'd not been straightforward with him. Then he closed the lid on the little cylindrical case and stowed it back into his trail sack.

I felt uncomfortable, so I tried changing the subject. "Are you going to head back down the trail now?" I asked.

"No," he answered

That was totally unexpected. "You mean you're just going to ride up the trail and head back down on the forest service road?"

"Yes," he asserted mildly.

What's the point of that? I wondered to myself. It all seemed very odd to me. *Why would he take the boring road instead of the miles and miles of premier singletrack?*

The three of us chatted for a few more minutes then the man put his helmet back on and said goodbye. He slowly guided his bike to the edge of the clearing before mounting it and turning left on the forest service road, heading in the direction that led down the mountain. Just as he disappeared from sight it *really* started to rain—not the steady drizzle we'd grown accustomed to, but weighty drops of water that announced their arrival with audible *plops* as they struck the forest flora. We looked up and could see the sky had become darker.

"Let's roll," Brian said in deference to the changing weather pattern. We geared up and took off, but not before lowering our seat posts for the long descent ahead.

The track was wet and slow in spots and required more pedaling than I thought it would. The first time I applied significant force to the downstroke I got the distinctive tingling in my legs that indicated I was going to cramp up. When I let off and started rolling under the momentum I'd generated, the tingling became more intense, like tiny spasmodic tears ripping through the muscle fibers of my legs. I shifted the pedals around to alternate which foot was forward in an attempt to introduce enough variety in my stance to ward them off. I even tried sitting back in my seat and taking my feet off the pedals, extending both legs forward, but that did not seem to help either. Yet, we kept rolling on, with me trying my best to keep up with Brian, but he kept getting further and further ahead of me. Thinking back to the encounter with the white-haired man, I started to regret not accepting his offer for a dose of the anti-cramp medicine.

At length I ran out of foot, pedal, and leg configurations to keep the cramps at bay, and my quads and hamstrings seized up a hundred times worse than the time four years ago when we biked off the mountain in Ketchum, Idaho, just before seeking solace at the hot springs. I yelled at Brian to stop, the distress in my voice reverberating through the woods like a flock of startled birds. I let the bike roll out from under my stiff-legged stance and hobbled over to the bank and lowered by rear end against it, my palms furiously rubbing each leg to try to release the tension that held them locked out.

The rainfall intensified, adding urgency to the need to keep on moving, but I wasn't able to go anywhere. I hated that I had interrupted the fun for Brian and I searched his face for any telltale signs of irritation or exasperation, but none was there. After about five minutes the pain subsided and I took that as a sign that the cramps were going away, so I told Brian I thought I was going to be okay now.

I pushed myself away from the bank and picked up my bike, but as soon as I got my feet back onto the pedals, both legs seized up again and I lurched back off the frame. We waited some more—five, ten minutes, I couldn't tell. Every moment of the pain felt like an hour. As the rain continued to move in and the sky steadily darkened, I realized that we only had a limited amount of daylight hours left, and neither one of us were equipped to ride in the dark.

I checked the GPS: we were just over three miles into the trail with nine miles to go. I hated to think what would happen if I got deeper into the remoteness of the trail and the cramps still incapacitated me. If I bailed out now, I could probably make it back to the clearing with the road grader where Brian could come and pick me up. It seemed like that option carried a lot more certainty of success than the alternatives I might face if the cramps kept up and we were another three to five miles deeper into the trail.

Brian was silent, looking upon my suffering with much bewilderment in his face, perhaps internally conflicted about what to do. "You're going to have to go on without me," I said. "I'm going to walk back out to the trailhead. When you get down the mountain come back up and pick me up there."

"You sure you'll be all right? Brian asked, his voice betraying his reluctance to leave me behind.

Brian had an analytical mind like me, so I knew what to say to assure him. "Look, we were about thirty minutes into the trail when we got here. Assuming you keep riding at that rate for the next nine miles, you should reach the bottom of trail in about an hour and a half. Then you have a half-hour drive up the mountain on top of that. That gives me two hours to backtrack the three miles to get out of here and wait for you at the trailhead. I ought to be able to manage one and a half miles an hour even if the cramps don't go away."

I could tell it made perfect sense to Brian, but I could also see he was torn between wanting to ride yet not wanting to abandon me, so I tacked on some assertive encouragement. "Go on, it's our best option. I'll be waiting for you back at the trailhead. Here, take the GPS. You'll need it more than I will."

Brian took the GPS and mounted his bike, then quickly disappeared into the forest. A great wave of disappointment swept over me as I realized this much-anticipated ride was not going to happen.

Lumbering, I pivoted the bike around on its rear wheel until the front pointed uphill. Leaning heavily on the handlebars, I started pushing up the trail, my still-cramped legs stretched out behind me, doing the best I could to move in a locked-out condition. A couple of times the cramps seemed to fade, and I'd try mounting my bike again to see if I could pedal, but that only brought on a fresh onslaught of pain.

After about forty-five minutes of struggling up the muddy track, I saw three bikers approaching. Seeing that I was pushing instead of riding, they stopped and asked if I had a flat. I briefly explained my situation, trying to minimize any concern, and they were soon on their way. Just before they took off I asked them if they knew how far it was from the trailhead.

"About a mile and a half," one of them responded.

I was making good progress and was relieved to know I would get back to the trailhead before Brian. Somewhat encouraged, I plodded onward. While the cramps were starting to abate—again—I'd learned my lesson after the other several false starts and stayed off the bike. Gradually walking became more normal, and by the time I reached the trailhead the cramps were gone.

Swarms of raindrops fell all around me, a persistently soaking downfall that showed no signs of letting up. I walked over to the grader and climbed up on it, thinking I could get shelter inside the cab, but the door was locked. I pushed my bike around the perimeter of the parking lot and finally saw a tamarack tree large enough to sit under. I laid down my bike and lowered myself carefully onto the damp ground, facing the parking lot. I ate my last energy bar, figuring I would need it to keep the internal fires burning to combat the damp and the chill.

It was quiet under that tree, and the falling drops of rain took on a soothing pattern as they landed on the forest floor around me. I started praying, first to exercise my faith by thanking God for the good he was working out of this event, no matter how crappy and disappointed I felt at the moment. Then my prayers started expanding toward more universal concerns. I prayed for revival in our land, then for his providence over the outcome of the upcoming presidential election, and then many other things that I can't specifically remember.

At any rate, I prayed for so long that it was almost as if I had worked myself into a trance, lost in the ambience of the surroundings. Then a drop of water hit me on the shoulder, then another one landed on my head. I drifted out of my prayerful state and realized the rain was beating down hard now, working its way through the overhead layers of branches and splattering random drops on various parts of my body. Reflexively, I put my helmet back on to help keep the water off my head and checked the time.

About two hours had elapsed since Brian and I had taken off in opposite directions. It was now 3:00 p.m. and for the first time all day I felt cold. I then realized how much heavier my water-soaked clothes had become, and I began to get concerned about hypothermia. *I should be up and moving about,* I told myself. *Trying to generate some body heat.* I figured I could hold out for a little bit longer, thinking it was so close to the time when Brian should arrive with his van, but if he wasn't back within the next half hour, I would head off the mountain.

I waited with my eye on my wristwatch, and got colder and colder. At 3:15 p.m. I realized it was becoming foolhardy to wait any longer. I had started shivering and was convinced that the early stages of hypothermia had indeed started to set in. I needed to move now or else there was a chance I might not survive.

I crawled out from under the tree, strapped on my CamelBak and took off. My legs felt like they were going to seize up on me again, but fortunately I didn't have to pedal very long or very much, as the downward slope of the forest road propelled me forward. Turning down the main forest service road that Brian and I had cranked up just a few hours ago, my bike rolled forward like a charging leopard. I clasped the brake handles with frigid fingers to keep control, enduring a burst of speed every time I eased up on the grip to relieve the pain in my hands. Mud kept slinging up in front and behind me, and I could taste the gritty, slimy clay whenever a gob landed in my mouth.

I was not quite halfway down the mountain when I rounded a curve and saw Brian's van heading toward me. Brian must have been awfully alert to recognize me so quickly and immediately stop. I slid to a halt next to him, full of joy upon seeing him. I opened the sliding side door and felt a deluge of warmth pour out of the van's interior. The gym bag with my change of clothes was on the floor behind the middle seat, and I stripped out of my soggy biking gear there by the side of the car.

"There's a towel in the back if you need one," Brian said as he mounted my bike onto the rack.

"Got it. Thanks."

When I finished changing I slammed the sliding door shut and climbed into the front seat, exulting in the blast of hot air from the heater. Brian got in and continued driving up the mountain until he'd found a place in the road wide enough to turn around so we could head back down. Eventually, we reached the lower trailhead where Brian dropped me off so I could get the Xterra. We decided to transfer my bike later.

Brian followed me out along Mission Creek Road, back through Cashmere, then back on Highway 97 to Wenatchee, where we turned off onto Highway 28. By the time we got to Quincy it had stopped raining, so I called Brian to suggest that we stop for food. I saw a Mexican restaurant coming up ahead and asked what he thought about eating there, and he said, "Sounds good."

The restaurant was empty except for two men playing pool near the center of the room. Above the counter seating area a TV on the wall flickered with black and white images of an old Mexican vampire movie. The Spanish-speaking actors spoke hyperdramatically, their scenes punctuated with crescendo-like blasts from an orchestra heavily staffed with brass instruments. This cacophonic mixture of dialogue and music was the loudest noise in the room until one of the men playing pool went over and fed some money into the jukebox, poked at a numeric keypad, then stepped back to the pool table as a spirited mariachi tune out-decibeled every other sound in the restaurant.

Our server arrived and we shouted out our food orders to her in Spanish, trying to blend in with the surroundings in both volume and idiom. She left and, since it was too loud to talk, we sat in silence. Brian cased out the restaurant while I thought about what happened today. I started to believe that somehow the whole fiasco had some spiritual meaning to it. I tumbled the idea around in my head through the series of songs blasting from the jukebox, when suddenly it went silent and all we could hear was the clacking of pool balls, as our server had turned the TV off during the thunderous musical interlude. Anyway, now we could talk—and eat, too, for the hot plates of Mexican comfort food had arrived.

In between large bites of a burrito, I started to verbalize the thoughts that had been running through my head while the jukebox had been blaring, hoping they coalesce them into something meaningful and coherent. "You know, what happened today would make a good story in a book. I mean, like how the elements of our ride were like the elements of our faith."

Brian looked at me as he chewed on a big chunk of chimichanga. His mouth was too full to speak, but the eager expression on his face indicated he wanted me to continue.

My thesis wasn't very well formed, but I ventured on anyway. "Well, our trail map is like the Bible. It tells us where we need to go to make our journey. In a Biblical sense, our journey through life. And the GPS is like the Holy Spirit, giving us moment by moment insight on how well we are staying true to the path and whether we are straying off course. And the energy bars are like the bread of life, sustaining us and renewing us along the way."

"And the rain is like the blood of Jesus, washing away our sins," Brian chimed in, now that he had swallowed his food.

"Yeah."

"So what would the trail be?" Brian asked.

"I don't know. I haven't gotten that far with the idea."

We continued eating our meal as we thought about the question. I never came up with an answer.

"You should write that book," Brian encouraged.

"Yeah," I said wistfully, as the vision started to take root. "I could call it 'Lessons from the Trail' and use a bunch more of our experiences. I could call the chapter based on today's experiences, 'Elements.'"

Brian's face brightened enough to lighten the dim atmosphere of the restaurant. "You could use that story you told me about Fields Spring, too," he enthused, apparently delighted to be a contributor to the book's genesis.

"Yeah, I could," I confirmed, letting his idea grip hold of me.

"Cool!" *Cool* was Brian's favorite exclamation and his tacit approval made me anxious to write "Elements" so he could read it. The next day I started working on a first draft, which was mainly just setting to ink everything I could remember that happened the day before. I finished it before the week was done and then put it aside.

I worked on the book off and on over the next seven years, documenting several more adventures during that time, and every now and then going back to "Elements" to touch it up. In January of 2014, I felt the writing was in decent enough shape to let someone else read it. Naturally, that someone else was Brian, since he was in most of the stories.

"Sometime I'd like for you to read some of the chapters I've written for my *Lessons from the Trail* book," I wrote to him. "Mainly to keep me honest!"

"You bet," he responded. "Send it over whenever."

Before I could follow through, though, I had second thoughts about "Elements" being ready to share, so I made up my mind to rework it. When Brian asked about where the book was a few weeks later, I appealed to his patience so I could take one more swing at improving that chapter, then I would send it along with the rest of the material.

It soon became clear to me as I worked on the next rewrite that "Elements" as a title subject was simply not going to work. For those folks steeped in sacramental theology, it would probably engender confusion at best and disapproval at worst, as elements are traditionally defined as water, bread, and wine. I was including the Bible and the Holy Spirit in the mix, definitely not elements in the traditional sense (and I hadn't even thought of something to correspond to wine). Besides, it started to become clear that the point of the adventure that day was not comparing the environmental elements to the elements of Christian faith, but faith itself.

When I told Brian to finish the Devil's Gulch trail without me, it never, ever occurred to me that he might not make it. Consider this: Brian would be travelling alone across twelve miles of never-before-seen trail in remote backcountry. He faced the potential of having mechanical issues or an accident, or even the possibility of coming to a crucial junction in the trail and making a wrong turn and getting lost. If any one of those things were to happen, then Brian's well-being would be in jeopardy.

Yet, I just knew that Brian was going to make it to the bottom of the trail and come back up the mountain to get me. In fact, of all the things I prayed for while seated under the tamarack tree waiting for him, not one prayer was offered asking God to help him make it to the end of the trail and back up the mountain. I never doubted that he would, so it never occurred to me that I needed to make that specific prayer request.

And yet Brian was just as fallible on that day as was any other human. In fact, on our next attempt at Devil's Gulch a year later, it would be Brian that would become incapacitated to the point of not being able to move (stomach cramps, which he blamed on a high-tech energy drink I let him try before we started up the mountain).

We never even reached the trailhead that day, as we had to abort that attempt halfway up the forest service road.

So, if I can have so much faith in an imperfect human being on an uncertain and somewhat precarious mountain-biking trail, why do I still sometimes struggle with faith in the God who is the creator of the entire universe, the primary force behind all existence? Is it because I can see a friend acting on my behalf, but I can't see God doing the same?

Countless times I'd seen Brian ride and I knew what his skills and physical capabilities were, so it was easy for me to trust he would make it back to his van and return to get me. I can't see God taking direct action on my behalf, but the Bible tells me what His skills are, and they are impeccable! How else to explain the many times in my life when I've undergone a trial or some form of suffering, only to have it become obvious years later that God was working on my behalf all during the ordeal. His skill at delivering His people is just as manifest today as it was some 3,500 years ago during the exodus out of Egypt.

I also think part of the struggle of keeping my faith in God lies in my ability to grasp the finite better than the infinite. God is always there, always true to his promises, always in a position to be counted on. But because He is God, He can't be predicted, and won't be limited by my meager expectations of how things ought to turn out when I go to Him for help in times of need. Instead, I have to be alert and respond to His way of reaching out to me. I think Moses must have understood that, since he plowed forward with the Israelites in tow when the waters of the Red Sea parted, instead of waiting for something familiar to show up that would allow him to cross, like a large boat.

Which brings me to the old man with the white hair whom we encountered just before we started our descent. I wonder if he hadn't been an angel sent by God to give me exactly what I needed before I even knew I needed it? Obviously I missed out because I could not *behold the moment* and respond accordingly. How else do you explain an individual whose predominant coloring is white, appearing as if out of nowhere, not making any sense about which way he was riding, but offering me the very remedy I would have willingly traded my bike for thirty minutes later?

Keeping steadfast in my faith in God means constantly giving up what I want to happen, or what I think should happen, and allowing whatever His will is to happen. That's easy to say, but tough to do. I know what I want and, in my pride, I think I know better than God on what needs to occur in order for me to get it. Thus, I'll trust myself or some other agent that I'm familiar with to help me get it before realizing I need to trust God to provide. I forget that what I think I know is good for me is but a breath on a windowpane compared to His knowledge of what is good for me.

It was good to have faith in Brian that afternoon on the Devil's Gulch. After all, he came through—somewhat heroically, in my book—but in reality I failed to realize that Brian wouldn't always be around. It would have been better to have placed that faith in God and develop the spiritual muscle that He wants me to have no matter where I am, whatever happens, who I'm with, or what I do.

THE WILDERNESS

It was time for Bob to head back to Clarkston, so we finished our coffee and then said goodbye to one another. On the walk back to the office I reminisced over his story about Brian. While his question about whether he would survive the ride with Brian had prompted the memory of the trip to Devil's Gulch, it was Bob's other question that began to resonate in my thoughts: *Where is this guy taking me?* It was starting to become apparent to me that Brian's departure from planet Earth was opening up a whole new trail for a lot of us to travel, and we were only just getting started.

I think that realization helped me see the futility in trying to keep plugging along with my current work demands and commitments as if they were sacrosanct. I was facing a different and far more important challenge that needed my full attention. Without any further hesitation I composed an email to my boss telling him I would be taking the day off tomorrow. In my heart I knew I needed to process in prayer what was happening and to think about what I should say this Saturday when I had to speak at Brian's memorial service.

After another visit to the hospital, where I helped get a hotel room for Amber and Alicia so they could take a break from having to stay on the eleventh floor, I arrived home more exhausted than I was the night before. I had absolutely no energy to think, much less to write, but I knew I needed to do a few more emails to some of Brian's other friends, plus update Zack on how the weekend was shaping up.

"Are you still thinking about coming over from Seattle this weekend?" I asked.

"Yeah," Zack replied. "Actually, I'm going to ask my boss if I can take Friday off and then drive over Thursday night after work." Zack lived in Seattle and was a civilian employee of the Navy assigned to the shipyard in Bremerton. He biked and took the ferry to work, so he was facing at least six hours of travel time to get to our home in Spokane.

"I hope he lets you, since I'd like to head down to Lewiston on Friday afternoon and spend the night there so I don't have to feel rushed Saturday morning trying to get to the memorial service," I explained. "Would you like to ride down with me?"

"Yeah, sure," he said.

I took great comfort from the benevolent spirit my son displayed. He was demonstrating a willingness to sacrifice his time and money to be with me during this time of grief. I went to bed after we finished talking, feeling touched and proud at the same time.

I woke up Wednesday morning, made a cup of coffee, then sat down to read the Bible. I came across Luke 5:16 where it mentions that Jesus often withdrew into the wilderness to pray. *Hmm*, I thought, *maybe I should do the same.* Brian's memorial service was in three days and I hadn't written down a single word of what I should say, and I desperately needed comfort and guidance from the Holy Spirit in order to fulfill that obligation. I longed to draw close to God, and it occurred to me that Jesus was setting an example of how to eliminate distractions so that you could achieve intimacy in prayer.

Well, it's not the same as the Judean desert, but I do live next to a large wooded area interspersed with a few hiking trails, which can also be used for mountain biking if you really wanted to make a go of it. I hastily left the house in a quest to find a spot where I could pray, but just as I was about to step outside I turned around to fetch a piece of paper and a pen. I had a strong sense I was going to need it to record the thoughts that I had faith God was going to give to me when I asked him for help in putting together what to say for Brian's memorial service.

I hastened down the driveway and stepped onto a short path that crossed an easement and led to the woods. I walked for about ten minutes until I reached a spot on a trail that tucks back into a small draw. I'd stopped there several times before to take videos of the little stream that flows in the springtime, and in those instances I'd noticed that the noise of traffic from the county highway disappears at that particular spot. The only other intrusions to the solitude there are from the occasional airplanes flying overhead or locomotives grinding along the Union Pacific line that hugs the hillside a couple of miles away. On that morning the only sounds I heard were from the birds that filled the air with their distinctive melodies.

I stood in that peaceful spot and prayed aloud, pouring out my grief and my need for God's strength for the task ahead of me. God creates out of the shapeless void and, out of the jumbled, formless thoughts swirling through my mind, he solidified what I needed to do that Saturday: to bring glory to God, to honor Brian's memory, and to give comfort to his family and friends. In other words, by virtue of seeking to give God the glory He is due, it was to be an act of worship.

WORSHIP

Asotin Creek is a tributary of the Snake River with headwaters in the Blue Mountains in Southeastern Washington. Parallel to the stream's north fork is a fun out-and-back trail that unravels through a deep, quiet, and sometimes mysterious canyon which Brian and I frequently biked in the springtime, especially since it was so close to our homes in Lewiston and Clarkston. Nestled in the lowlands, the Asotin Creek Trail is often snow-free and ridable in early March, and is perfect for reacclimating to mountain biking after a winter-long hiatus.

The trail starts out relatively flat and obstacle-free but becomes steeper and more technical the further in it goes. As Brian and I saw it, the ultimate goal in riding the trail was to reach a flat and broad grassy area which we named the meadow—not the end point of the trail, but the most practical turnaround spot along its ten-mile length. We never got to the meadow on the first outing of the year, but each successive ride brought us closer and closer to it as our riding proficiency improved and enabled us to plunge deeper and deeper into the canyon. It was always reassuring to experience the restoration of our stamina and skills which had grown rusty from the lack of use during the off-season, knowing those things would prepare us to ride and enjoy the more robust trails we liked to do in the summer, like the ones on Moscow Mountain.

I don't know how common a mindset this is among mountain bikers, but for me, every trail offered the challenge for a perfect ride. That meant overcoming every single obstacle and challenge in the trail without losing control and wrecking or stalling out and having to get off the bike and push. I'd been riding the Asotin Creek Trail for about fifteen years and had yet to do it. Usually it took until May to get in good enough shape to complete the trip to the meadow, and maybe if I'd continued riding the trail through the summer I'd get enough practice to master the more difficult sections of the trail. However, at some point the temperature would heat up enough to coax the rattlesnakes to leave their dens and overrun the sections of the trail close to the creek. It only took one unwitting excursion into this multitude of slithering buzz bombs to convince me to retreat and never again set foot on the trail during hot weather.

Eager for another trip into the canyon and knowing that the trail conditions were peaking, Brian and I tried to hook-up for an after-work ride all throughout the second week of May. We kept running into conflicts, mostly with commitments to our kids' sporting endeavors, but a few grown-up activities as well. Saturday morning, usually the best time of the week to ride, was also booked with kids and sports, so we settled on Sunday morning, at daylight, with the intentions of getting a ride in and returning home in time to get cleaned up and head off to Sunday school and church.

We met at the trailhead where Lick Creek flows into Asotin Creek with a half hour of daybreak already behind us. After catching up on how our weekends were going, we attached our helmets and CamelBaks, straddled our bikes, and bowed our heads in prayer. "Dear God," Brian led off, "we thank you for this morning and the opportunity to ride. Keep us safe, keep our bikes working good, help us to have fun, and bring us safely back home to our families. In Jesus' name…"

"Yes, Lord," I added. "Help us to have a perfect ride and…" (because we hadn't reached it yet this year)… "help us make it to the meadow. Thank you for allowing us to get away and enjoy your creation this morning. In Jesus' name we pray, amen."

"Red-eye?" Brian asked.

"Ready," I replied, and we took off, wheeling around the green gate that keeps motorized vehicles off the trail, then down the bank and across the rushing waters of Lick Creek, dry most of the year, but now laden with snow melt from the top of the mountain.

Riding with Brian always had a subtle, competitive element about it, but in a good sort of way. If I was leading, I felt challenged to make sure I was going fast enough so that I wouldn't hold him up. If he was leading, I felt a similar obligation to not get so far behind that he would have to stop and wait for me. On that morning, I was the first to emerge from the Lick Creek crossing and so I became the pacesetter for the ride.

The trail started out as double track from an old jeep road, except for a fifty-foot section at the base of a rock cliff near the start where the flood of 1995 washed away half of it. When I reached that section, the water rushed by in a thrashing roar, and my bike frame trembled from the assault of the current along the creek bank. After that the trail began to wander away from the creek bed and into the woods, and the stream sounds gradually faded as more and more trees found a foothold at the bottom of the scraggly hillside. All in all it was an easy four miles of 1-3 percent gradient up to a cattle guard where the double track ended. I stopped there and waited for Brian to pull up alongside of me.

"That only took us twenty-three minutes," I announced after glancing at the timer on my sport watch.

"Wow! That was fast!" he exclaimed. "It was taking us about thirty-two minutes at the beginning of this year."

"Do you want to take the lead now?" I asked, knowing he would no longer have the opportunity to pass me if I was moving too slowly.

"Keep going," he encouraged. "You're doing a good job."

I clipped in and took off, intensifying my focus on the trail in anticipation of the technical sections that would soon appear. The natural springs that dotted the landscape just beyond the cattle guard were dry this year, so what was usually a sloppy slog through a marshy area was instead an easy go over solid land, giving us a clean and fast start on the singletrack that penetrated the more densely wooded area. Coming up were several steep climbs, hidden around the various gyrations in the trail, but we'd ridden the trail enough to know they were imminent. Before each hill came into sight we geared up a couple of notches to build some speed, then hit the base of the hill fast, shifting down as we climbed to maintain a constant tempo as we brute-forced over roots and around stones that threatened to slow us up and throw off our momentum.

After conquering the steep, technical hills we next approached an extremely rocky section, one that routinely doled out pinch-flats as punishment for underinflated tires. This had been a difficult section to master, but I finally figured out the trick to getting through it without stopping was to power a downstroke at each of the bulging, jagged edges of the irregularly-shaped stones while slightly lifting the front end of the bike. This involved concentration and impeccable timing, and fortunately I had both that morning as I made it through without being jostled to a halt by some of the larger chunks of rubble.

Continuing on our relentless trek toward the meadow, the rocky section soon yielded to a firmly packed segment of the trail, giving us a break from the hard work and allowing us to enjoy some fun as the twists, turns, and dips rolled swiftly underneath us. After that burst of riding bliss, I sensed it was time for refueling our muscles with some sports gels, so I pulled over alongside a simple structural landmark on the trail that we called the corral. The corral consisted of an upper and lower ring of debarked logs affixed at their ends to short cross-posts. We'd always assumed it was a makeshift holding pen, an artifact from a time long ago when free-range cattle regularly roamed the area. Now tall stalks of mature cattails filled the enclosure. In the center of the circle, one of the stalks vibrated back and forth like a tuning fork, and yet there was no wind around whatsoever.

"Look, Brian," I said, pointing. "I wonder what's causing that cattail to shake like that. None of the other ones are moving."

Brian stared long and hard at the area. "Huh!" he eventually grunted. "That's weird. Why do you think it's doing that?"

My analytical mind raced back to the wood biology class I'd taken in grad school. "Maybe it has something to do with water transport through the xylem...maybe the aquifer is bubbling up only under the center of the corral and that's why it's moving." As I struggled to build upon the fledging theory I'd just proffered, I began to wonder if it wasn't something supernatural, like a manifestation of God's presence. Something akin to Moses and the burning bush. Ike and Brian and the shaking stick, perhaps? I finished sucking down the gooey gel and continued to stare. Eventually I concluded it was just one of those things that made the canyon mysterious from time to time. I shrugged off my thoughts and then admitted, "Honestly, I don't know what's causing it."

We were silent for a few more moments, watching the cattail continue to sway back and forth, until Brian finally said, "We better get going."

"Yep," I agreed. "Can't forget we're on a schedule." I ceased my wonderment over the shaking stick and took off for the final climb to the meadow, cognizant that the strange event had started something stirring within me.

The ride up to the corral had gone well—better than any other trip up the canyon that I could remember—but now we were coming up on one of the most difficult spots to negotiate: the access to what we called the high trail, a section atop a 300-foot slope that drops precipitously down to where the creek flows like a silver ribbon. Getting on the high trail involved cranking up a deceptively steep pitch of dirt and overcoming a ledge formed by a flat and protruding boulder at the crest of the ascent. It wasn't often that we would make it far enough into the canyon to practice getting over this spot, and it had always been a stumbling block in each and every quest to reach the meadow. I approached the access to the high trail knowing there was a solid history of failure behind me in being able to successfully overcome this obstacle.

Despite the awareness of my past failures, I sensed confidence welling up in me, as if the strange stirring I had felt when we left the corral had imbued me with strength and wisdom to overcome what lay ahead. I prepared for the challenge by keeping the gear low and whirling my legs around like a high-speed eggbeater. Sure, it would have been more efficient to get that speed in a higher gear, like I was used to doing, but it occurred to me that the reason all my other attempts had not been successful was because the rapidly changing slope didn't allow enough time to shift down to the gear that allowed me to get the power needed to complete the climb over the boulder. For the first time, I understood that all my past failures were a result of struggling against too much torque to make it over the top, thus causing me to stall out and have to dismount.

As I neared the ledge, the rotational speed of my legs slowed but my heart rate soared into the red zone. While making one final, mighty push on the pedal, I pulled up the front end of the bike over the stony protuberance. Quickly—as timing was critical—I added two more rapid and powerful down strokes to get my rear wheel over the boulder, and the next thing I knew I was rolling on the high trail.

I felt exuberant! I had done something I had never before accomplished, and I felt my heart swell with joy over what I considered a significant victory. Then I heard Brian's gears shifting close behind me, which told me he'd managed to clear the boulder as well. It felt so good and right that we were both tracking so well.

I transitioned to a steady cadence, essential for keeping control on the narrow slice of singletrack high above the creek. We cruised to the apex of the high trail and then dropped down into a gully, using the momentum generated from the plunge to roll up the other side and land in the meadow. Our bikes coasted to a halt amid the tall grasses, completing what I knew was the first-ever perfect ride up Asotin Creek.

Then the unplanned and unexpected happened. The stirring feeling that began at the corral was now like rushing water within me and I could no longer contain it. As sweat rushed out of my pores, I threw off the bike, walked a few yards further into the meadow, then dropped onto my knees. I began to pray aloud, my hands rising toward the sky, pouring out heartfelt phrases of worship to the author of perfection, the one who had heard my prayer at the start and graciously allowed me to complete this unforgettable ride.

"Oh, God!" I shouted. "You are a great and magnificent God, the creator of all things, the author behind the beauty of this canyon and this morning. How good you are, and how perfect are your ways. Thank you for giving us the strength in our legs to make this trip, for the breath in our lungs, and the beating of our hearts to carry us on. Thank you for the technology you have given us to allow us to do what previous generations have never done. You are so good to us, so great in mercy, so powerful and almighty. You alone are worthy of our praise. I praise you, oh God, and thank you for all you have done!"

It didn't stop there. On and on I went, shouting our praises and thanks for things now that I can't remember, until I became mute from a loss for words. At that point silence filled the meadow, save for the breath of life flowing in and out of me with overwhelming gratitude. I started coming to my senses, becoming cognizant of what I had just spontaneously done, and I thought of Brian, whom I had not looked at since we arrived at the meadow. I became anxious, wondering how he was going to react to my exuberant outpouring of praise. Would he regard me as overly fanatical and want to make a cautious retreat from this solemn place of unfettered worship?

My apprehension turned to relief when I heard him begin to echo up similar praises. I listened humbly as his words validated what I had just felt and expressed, and I allowed the warmth in my heart to overflow with a greater love and appreciation to the God of all creation. I remained on the ground with my eyes closed and on my knees until Brian had finished, feeling so grateful to be alive and aware of God's magnificence, and so blessed to be able to share that with such a terrific friend and brother in Christ. One more offering of thanks and then I stood up and looked over at Brian, who was finishing his praise in silence, also on his knees in reverence before our awesome God. At last he stood.

"What an incredible God we have," I acknowledged solemnly.

"God is great. God is so good," Brian responded. What more could be said?

After another moment in silence, I said, "It's time to head back," and thus we shifted our thoughts from the eternal back to the temporal.

Propelled by our shared experience of worshipping God's glory in the depths of Asotin Creek Canyon, the ride back to the trailhead was an ecstatic blur of pleasure, mountain biking as if we were created to do it, and the expression of that purpose bringing us the sense of God's delight in us. I wanted the Asotin Creek Trail ride to never end, but it did much too quickly, as it seems like all good things do. We reached the trailhead, packed up our bikes and gear, and went our separate ways. Soon we would reunite with our families and make our way to our respective churches for worship. Needless to say, it would be nothing like the worship we experienced in the meadow.

In retrospect, it's a minor miracle that, after completing such a flawless ride, I didn't succumb to pride and begin to high-five Brian for what we had just done. That would be my normal, self-centered approach to celebrating something awesome. Amazingly, and solely by His grace, God imbued me that day with a spirit of wisdom which allowed me to see that our achievement was a gift from Him, and my bold expression of gratitude and praise for that realization allowed Brian to see it as well. The bikes, our physical capabilities, the majestic setting—it all pointed to the fact that we had been blessed to be witnesses and participants in something so glorious and sublime, so beyond our capacities to create and execute, and so unexpected in terms of the joy we felt when that truth was revealed to us. Worship was the right response to that revelation, the only response worthy of offering.

BATTLING SATAN'S DEVICES

My objectives were now clear for what I needed to do in preparing for Brian's memorial service, and I had a sense of purpose stronger than anything I had felt in years. I repeated the revelation several times there in the quiet spot, making sure I cemented those three objectives into my mind: to bring glory to God, to honor Brian's memory, and to give comfort to his family and friends. Then I prayed for God's Holy Spirit to give me the words to say to accomplish these three things.

When I had finished praying, I stood quietly there in the secluded draw, listening to the singing from two different species of birds, their antiphonal warblings punctuating the stillness around me. I emptied my mind of all other thoughts and waited for the words from God to formulate within. I must have held that position for about ten minutes when a silent, internal whisper said, "Go now."

A sliver of stubbornness inside of me objected, saying *No, I haven't gotten the words to say*, but it wasn't strong enough to keep me from being obedient. I started walking back home with no further indication of what to say to accomplish the purpose that had been set before me, but I had no anxiety or doubts about fulfilling that purpose. I felt excited about walking in faith with nothing but an inexplicable assurance that my prayer would be answered.

I was just over halfway home when all at once the hodgepodge of thoughts inside my head coalesced into a trove of meaningful ideas. I stopped and retrieved the pen and paper from my pocket and began the frantic process of transferring the ideas into written words. The impressions were coming so quickly that I could hardly keep up the pace of scribbling to capture them all. I had folded the paper three times to provide enough backing to prevent the tip of the pen from poking through as I wrote, and the first fold had filled up in no time. I flipped it over and covered up the backside with more words, then unfolded and refolded the rapidly filling sheet to write down even more. Within less than five minutes my handwriting had covered both sides of the paper, and I hastened to unfold and refold it so I could enumerate the order in which I'd written everything down before I could forget. God had rewarded my faith abundantly in one fell swoop, and I rushed home to begin fleshing out the outline that He'd given me in that burst of inspiration.

Upon returning home, I went into the study located in the front of our house. In there was an antique writing desk, the kind with a pivoting board that lowers from the desk face to form the working surface. Onto this slightly rickety piece of furniture I placed my laptop from work, similar to Brian's, and flipped it open. Just as I was about to hit the start button to boot it up, I hesitated. *What am I doing?* I thought to myself. *Who am I to speak words of hope and comfort at a time like this?*

Staring blankly ahead at the dark computer screen, I began to question my resolve about what I was setting out to do. A depression started settling in over me as I realized I was not worthy to speak on behalf of Brian or even witness to the glory of God. I became aware of my worst sins over my lifetime and how they were at risk of being exposed to everyone once I took to the platform at Brian's memorial service to commence delivering the message. The thought deepened my depression. I began to believe I had made a grave error in agreeing to speak, and the fear of potential humiliation paralyzed my will to proceed any further on the task that had been set before me. I felt crushed by the weight of guilt, sadness, and shame.

Unable to move anything but my eyes, I glanced over to my right and there, pushed aside to make room for my laptop, was a book I had purchased a month earlier but had not yet read. I'd heard about the book listening to a podcast by Timothy Keller, pastor of Redeemer Presbyterian Church in New York City. Getting and reading the book was a passing recommendation in the sermon Keller was delivering in the podcast, and it had nothing to do with the main point of his message, but for some reason I acted on it. The book was called, *Precious Remedies Against Satan's Devices* and was written over 350 years ago by Thomas Brooks, a Puritan preacher who lived in England.

It took an inordinate amount of energy to reach over and pick up the book. I started flipping through the pages until I saw a chapter heading titled, "Satan's Devices to Keep Saints in Sad Condition." The first device that Brooks lists in that chapter is "by causing us to remember our sin more than our Savior." I read the remedies to that then flipped forward to another chapter titled, "Satan's Devices to Keep Souls from their Holy Duties." Device #3 was "by presenting to the soul the difficulty of performing them." Both of these writings nailed exactly what I was going through at that moment, and I immediately understood that I was under a very palpable spiritual attack – the second skirmish that week, and just as intense as the first one experienced in the ICU waiting room the night of the accident.

Now I realized that what had been set before me to do was such an important task that it was an immense threat to the plans of Satan to the point that he was actively trying to bring me down and put me out of the game. I prayed to God for continued strength to fight the evil one, and thanked Him for the words that he had inspired Thomas Brooks to write that just saved my neck. I marveled at the extraordinary yet thorough orchestration of events that took place to have these remedies right next to me the exact moment I needed to hear them the most—from Brooks writing the book three and a half centuries ago in the first place, to Keller mentioning it in a podcast that I happened to listen to, which prompted me to buy the book, only to set it aside in at a place where it would be instantly available to me at a critical moment of need. Once again, here was God's sovereign hand in action, this time spanning centuries instead of years. So impressed was I with this remarkable glimpse into how He works that I instantly emerged from my dark despair, said a resounding "Amen!" and got to work.

I wrote out the framework of the message that morning, pretty much unencumbered by any other obligations. Shortly before noon, just as I was getting ready to take a break to go swimming at one of the city pools, I ran upstairs to check my home email on my Mac and saw where Jared had sent me Brian's "I Am Second" testimony which he had successfully extracted from Brian's damaged laptop hard drive. I was overwhelmed with gratitude, and again saw God's hand in my mortal affairs, this time by placing me in a work environment with a tech-savvy Christian whom I could turn to for help recovering the document. Before leaving, I quickly read through Brian's testimony then texted Aaron and a few other church members to let them know the good news.

I started editing Brian's testimony when I got back from the pool, focusing on fixing up some of the grammatical elements to help the text flow more smoothly. If I couldn't do that without altering the meaning of what he was trying to say, I left it alone. In one area Brian had phonetically written down the name of a type of jaw surgery he'd undergone many years ago, and it required quite a bit of online research to find the precise medical definition of what he was trying to describe. I felt the extra work was worth it since Brian was trying to make the point that breaking his jaw to fix his condition was emblematic of him needing to break his backsliding ways as a half-committed Christian.

I finished the editing work and as I went to save the revised version of Brian's "I Am Second" testimony, I saw a file named "BMJ Emails," a document I had created back in September 2008 and had last updated in June 2009. It was a record of all the emails Brian and I had exchanged at work since 2006. There were several hundred of them, and in an effort to clean up my inbox at work but not lose the content of these emails, I had copied and pasted them over into a Word document, since they preserved records of our many adventures together and the events that led up to them. They also documented some of the spiritual struggles and victories we'd undergone in our individual pursuits, along with some of the normal ups and downs of life in general.

When I became the vice-president of my company's information technology group, I scaled back the number of interoffice emails between us, figuring it wasn't setting a very good example to be spending so much time on personal communications while at work.

Now I regretted that decision, especially when I considered how much work had intruded into my personal life over the course of my career—far, far more than my personal life had intruded upon work—and how much I valued Brian's messages now that he was gone.

After saving the latest version of "I Am Second," I opened "BMJ Emails" so I could update the document with the emails we'd exchanged from my home account. It wasn't long before I came across the email where I had asked Brian if he wanted to read the chapters I'd written so far in "Lessons from the Trail." Even though he'd said to send them on, I never got any of them to him. *He would have loved reading these,* I thought. *And now he can't.*

The regret I felt at that moment was visceral, as if a sinkhole had formed in my heart and my entire being was collapsing into it. The stories were probably good enough to share at the time, but in the vain pursuit of perfection I had missed an opportunity to stoke memories that would have surely brightened Brian's day and brought a smile to his face. It made me realize the foolishness in withholding things from your loved ones because you think those things aren't good enough, when in reality it's the gesture and the process that matters more. I treasured those memories of our rides and had really wanted to share them with Brian, but now it would never happen. What good is a treasure if there is no one to share it with?

TREASURE

The scent of bacon sizzling in the frying pan woke me up out of a deep slumber, maybe the first time the sense of smell had ever roused me from my sleep. Breakfast beckoned, but I was too tired to even open my eyes, much less get out of bed. It had been a long and rough week at work, and I had to stay up way too late on Thursday night to get ready for the adventure that Brian and I had planned for the weekend in the Payette National Forest in Central Idaho. I left Spokane directly from work on Friday afternoon, drove two hours to meet Brian in Lewiston, then we drove another three hours to McCall, Idaho, to meet up with some of Brian's church friends at a cabin on the eastern shore of Payette Lake. Needless to say, it was very late by the time we got to bed, so despite the aroma of food enticing me to get up and eat, I gave into the bone crushing fatigue, rolled over in the bunk bed and covered my face with a pillow. Boy would it be nice to get some more sleep!

As I started to drift off, I began thinking about the adventure that we had planned for the day and what we hoped to accomplish. It was going to be an epic ride, that much was for sure, as we had plotted out a sixteen-mile round trip to a small body of water called Loon Lake. What we hoped to accomplish on the ride, though, was to locate the remains of an airplane wreckage dating back to World War II.

Imagine this: It's the winter of 1943 and you are one of eight crewmembers of a B-23 Dragon Bomber returning from a training mission in Nevada. As you listen to the steady drone of the engine, your thoughts are on the war being waged in Europe and in the Pacific and how your training might be deployed under actual combat conditions. Looking through the cockpit window, you see the vast expanse of the Payette National Forest beneath you, a 2.3 million-acre jewel of rugged mountains, high-alpine meadows, vast forests and jaw-dropping deep river canyons all covered in an unrelenting whiteness of tons and tons of snow. Suddenly, the predictable hum of the plane's motor changes. The sounds are distressed, and you begin to fight off the sense of panic that is rumbling in your gut. Fortunately, the pilot is skilled enough to bring the plane down safely onto the frozen waters of Loon Lake, about twenty-two miles northeast of McCall, Idaho.

The plane skids across the icy surface and lands about 150 feet in from the southern shore, shearing off both of its wings in the process. After you get over the initial jolt of the landing, you check to see if everyone is all right and discover that your seven crewmates have all survived, with the worst injury among you being a soldier with a broken knee. You wait five days hoping to see a search plane, but the silent skies eventually convince you that you and your crewmates alone will have to be responsible for your rescue. You agree to be one of the three who set out on the long and uncertain trek toward civilization. In the span of fourteen days you hike forty-two miles through waist deep snow until you reached the Lake Fork Guard Station where one of your fellow men pick up the phone there in the station and reach an operator in McCall. Four days later, a search plane arrives and spots the wreckage, and within another four days every man among you is rescued safely back to civilization.

Just as my thoughts of the men aboard the B-23 were morphing into a dream, I heard a loud voice: "Breakfast is ready!" This time as I stirred back awake I could smell fresh coffee along with the other odors of food, and that was enough to get me out of my sleeping bag and staggering toward the kitchen. Jim Gentry, one of Brian's friends and the cabin owner, was standing by the stove with a spatula in hand, building a stack of pancakes onto a plate. Moments later, Brian and his other friend, Gary Thorne, appeared, both eager to partake of Jim's huge repast of pancakes, eggs, bacon, and toast. We devoured it heartily, stuffing down as much as we could to fuel up for the ride ahead.

During breakfast, Brian and I reviewed the plan with Jim and Gary for how we would execute the ride. I'd ridden the trail before to

Loon Lake (but had not made it to the wreckage), so I was somewhat familiar with what to expect and how best to manage the trip. "We should put in at Ruby Meadows campground and come out at the Chinook campground at the end of Warren Wagon Road," I said. (Warren Wagon is the main road out of McCall to the recreational areas north of Payette Lake.) "That will knock off about eight miles of pedaling along a boring, dusty road," I added as a selling point.

Then Brian spoke up. "We'll have to shuttle. Gary, can you take your car to Chinook?"

"Yes," he answered.

"Ok," Brian continued. "We'll put all our bikes on the top of my car, follow you there and pick you up, then head back to Ruby Meadows."

"Sounds like a plan," said Jim.

After we'd finished breakfast we headed out the cabin and started loading the bikes into the quad carrier on top of Brian's van. That's when I noticed Gary's bike looked more like a road bike than a mountain bike. In fact, it looked like a very fragile road bike, an impression enhanced by the pastel color of the frame. It reminded me more of what you would see rolling lazily along a beach boardwalk than something that would traverse singletrack in a rugged pristine forest.

"How do you think my bike's going to do on the trail?" Gary asked Brian and me.

"Well," I ventured, trying not to sound discouraging, "it will probably be a little bumpy on the rougher sections of the trail since you don't have a front and rear suspension."

Brian chimed in. "You're going to have a challenge climbing without a lower gear set, but you do a lot of road biking on the hills around Lewiston and Clarkston so maybe it won't be a big deal."

One thing I did not voice was my skepticism about the bike's durability. It simply did not look rugged enough to match the terrain we were about to ride on. Gary was a good road rider, and *maybe* he *could* make it, but I sure would not have taken that kind of bike onto the trail.

We left Jim's cabin and headed north on Warren Wagon Road. It took over an hour to get to Chinook Campground where we dropped off Gary's car and then backtracked to Ruby Meadows, where we unloaded our bikes. After strapping on our helmets and CamelBaks, Brian led us in prayer before we took off through the campground to the start of the trail.

It was a smooth and gentle climb during the first mile or so, followed by an equal measure of descent. Then we encountered some more climbing before hitting a fast section that segued into some roller coaster sections, where the trail builders had put in some nice banks to allow you to take the turns swiftly. The forest service maintenance crew had also done a good job by keeping the trail clear of debris, as we didn't once have to get off our bikes to climb over fallen timber. We passed through an old burn area and then through some low-lying swamps, rolling over low-lying wooden bridges constructed to protect the habitat. Then there were the inevitable rocky sections that created challenges, especially for Gary.

Gary's frustration with his bike and the journey became more and more manifest each time we stopped to let everyone regroup. He wrecked once and was having trouble maintaining control of his bike at the speeds the descents naturally lent themselves to, so he was constantly holding back. The ankle injury from the wreck was also starting to get painful and distracting, and he was beginning to talk about heading back.

We had one more ascent of about 600 feet before getting to Loon Lake. Normally this would not have been too much trouble for me, but by the end of the climb I was suddenly feeling very tired. Discouragement quickly followed, as if I'd been devastated with a sudden depression, a loss of will to continue on. I grappled trying to understand the intensity of this sudden and unexpected emotion. Perhaps the weeklong accumulation of stress at work compounded with insufficient sleep had reached a tipping point and overwhelmed my central nervous system. At any rate, when Gary finally showed up at the junction of the Look Lake and Chinook Campground Trails and announced he was going back, I felt very sympathetic. *Maybe I should go with him,* I thought, half out of the hopelessness I felt about continuing in the present physical condition in which I found myself and half out of concern for Gary's well being.

Jim immediately tried to talk Gary out of it, but Gary was insistent. Jim, channeling his former school-teacher's voice, used persuasive words of encouragement, like, "You've come this far, you can go a little more," versus Gary, a rational medical doctor by profession, describing the pain from the injury in detail and the demerits of proceeding on such a poor choice of bicycle. Gary eventually prevailed in their argument, insisting he had just enough reserve to make it back, and he turned and started up toward the trail heading to the Chinook Campground, where he would wait for us to return.

I was almost ready to say I was going back, too, when Jim asked Brian, "You're going on, right?"

"Yep," Brian replied without hesitation.

"Ike?" Jim asked, looking at me.

I nodded yes, but did not speak the word, because I could not bring myself to say yes when my entire flesh was ganging up on me to turn back. Now I was compelled to act out of commitment to my word, even though I did not think I could make it. If there was a faint glimmer of hope inside of me that suggested I could keep going, I sure didn't sense it.

The three of us started down the Loon Lake trail, and in less than a minute we met a quartet of bikers heading toward the trail junction. We stopped to chat and learned they had biked to see the B-23 a year ago. They pointed to the area of the lake where we would find the wreckage, adding that we would have to wade across a stream to get there. I peered in the distance where they pointed, wondering if I could catch a glint of glimmering metal from the wreckage to help pinpoint the location, but all I saw was shoreline. We thanked them for the info and headed on.

The next section of the trail reinforced the idea that I had made the wrong decision to keep going. The trail was littered with an assortment of rocks ranging from large to monolithic, and I didn't have even a spark of energy to concentrate on how best to navigate around these obstacles, much less actually do it with the bike. My legs felt heavy and useless, like they'd devolved into sluggish blobs of protoplasm.

With almost zero drive left within me, I was close to giving up, but a sudden yelp from Jim broke this debilitating self-absorption. I lifted my head in time to catch a glimpse of Jim's feet pointing skyward as the rest of his torso headed over the bank behind a large outcropping of granite boulders. Brian jumped off his bike and scrambled down the bank to check on him while I ditched my bike and ran to the scene as well. Jim emerged up from the bank on his own accord, somewhat shaken up, but grateful that he had his helmet on. After that mishap, we reasoned it was better if we pushed our bikes through the rest of the jumbled outcropping of rocks and boulders until they cleared up.

I noticed then that I wasn't hopelessly fatigued any more. The adrenaline rush from witnessing Jim's accident and responding to it must have energized me for the moment, as if I were a video game character whose shrinking life meter suddenly got restored in full after finding a magic potion. Then I remembered: I *had* packed a magic potion—well, actually a potent fat burner pill—in my CamelBak. Supplement companies sell all kinds of capsules and tablets labeled as fat burners, some with exotic ingredients, but mostly all of them contain caffeine. They are perfect on the trail when you need a boost of energy to keep on riding or extra focus to make that last, long downhill descent. If only I could take one, I thought, maybe I could make it the rest of the way.

We rode on for about ten more minutes, then Brian pulled off the trail toward a primitive campsite near the general area where the quartet of bikers had pointed. We knew that the last part of the journey to the B-23 was best done on foot, and Brian thought the campsite looked like a good spot to ditch the bikes. I pulled in last and let my bike keel over to the ground, sort of symbolic of how I felt once I'd dismounted. I did not want to tell Brian or Jim I was going to take a fat burner, so I just said I needed to get something out of my CamelBak and would catch up with them.

Brian and Jim went ahead, stripping down to their biking shorts and crossing the narrow stream that flowed into the northeast corner of Loon Lake. Both of them made funny gasping noises each time the water level reached a certain landmark on their anatomy. I watched Brian wade across first, carrying his shoes and jersey overhead, then Jim followed, carrying the same plus a small digital camera.

By the time Jim had completed crossing the stream I'd found the small container that held the fat burner with 200 mg of caffeine in it. I watched them put their shoes and jerseys back on as I popped the pill into my mouth then inserted the end of the CamelBak's sipper tube into my mouth and sucked the pill down with the flow of water. Then I stripped, and waded into the water. As my feet traversed the sandy bottom and the cold and steadily moving stream inched its way up to my chest, I found myself making the same shivering sounds that Brian and Jim had made when they crossed.

I scuttled up the stream bank only to find Brian and Jim had managed to put a fair amount of distance between me and them and now appeared to be just on the perimeter of a burn area. Maybe it was the immersion into the cold water, or maybe the fat burner had kicked in a lot faster than normal, but I suddenly felt energetic and began bounding through the underbrush and jumping over fallen logs as I hustled to catch up. It wasn't long before the ground had gradually sloped down into shallow marsh area covered with lily pads. I was gaining ground on them and was soon less than the length of a football field away when what I beheld caused me to freeze in my tracks.

I could not believe the chromatic intensity of the scene before my eyes. Three striking colors dominated my entire field of view: the deep emerald green of the blanket of lily-pads, the multitude of vertical white stripes formed by the bleached remains of the tall conifers comprising the burn area, rising like ivory tusks from an ancient graveyard of gigantic wooly mammoths, and the cloudless deep blue sky hovering over the scene like the inside of a sapphire umbrella. Punctuating this triad of hues, and neatly framed by the towering tree skeletons, were the human figures of Brian and Jim, with Brian's bike jersey looking like the red and white stripes of the Peruvian flag. The color and composition of the scene was at once beautiful and surreal, like an elaborately staged dream sequence in a foreign film, but so vast in scale and unimaginable in execution that it pointed to God as the stage director. I lingered for as long as I could savor the beauty of the moment, but then I had to start running through the swamp again to catch up with Brian and Jim, who were still trekking onward, oblivious of their role in creating such a stunning vista.

"You should have seen yourselves just now," I called out as I got closer.

"What?" they asked in unison.

I tried to explain what I had just witnessed, but I don't think it registered. They were focused on finding the B-23, not on aesthetics, so I resigned myself to the fact that this once-in-a-lifetime vision of God's artistic perfection in this particular setting was a gift to me and me alone. Transcendent moments are as ephemeral as a stunning sunset, so I said a quick prayer of thanks and rejoined Brian and Jim in the search.

We turned toward the direction of the lake, trudging through ankle-deep water but occasionally coming up on small berms of dry land. Responding to a gut feeling, I veered off toward northeast where I sensed the wreckage would be. Brian and Jim followed me and eventually we came to a clearing where we sighted the heap of grey metal that seemed so obviously out of place in this pristine wilderness. Overjoyed, the three of us started shouting and running full tilt as we quickly descended upon the crash site.

We looked in amazement at the artifact before us, circling the lump of metal with our imaginations running rampant as we tried to fathom what it must have been like to have been in the plane when it went down at this spot in 1943. I moved closer and touched the fuselage, running my fingers across the dulled metal surface and feeling the absorbed warmth of the overhead sun. I felt the parts of the exposed engine, motionless for the past sixty-six years, wondering if it could ever fire up again. Lastly, I looked at the battered instrument panel in the cockpit, trying to imagine I was the pilot having to respond to the signals that indicated the plane was going down.

Jim set up the timer on his camera for a group picture and we huddled in front of the plane and played up some manly poses as the shutter clicked. Then we raced to the lake's rim and found the pair of wings that had been sheared off when they hit the trees. In short, we lost ourselves in the activities of our youth, behaving as if we were elementary school boys play-acting an adventure. It was a treasure hunt, one that culminated not in the discovery of material riches, but in rekindling a long-lost feeling of joy and wonderment.

Hours later, after we'd completed the grunt-inducing climb out of Loon Lake to the Chinook Campground Trailhead, we high-tailed it to Bergdorf Hot Springs to soak away the soreness in our quads, hams, and glutes. Lazing across the floating log that the owners kept in the pool, Brian talked about how much he already wanted to come back and take his three daughters to see the B-23, maybe even get another friend to come with him and bring his kids. I sighed as the thermal waters drew out all the aches and pains in my body and looked up into the sky, still infinitely blue, and thanked God for such a perfect day.

Later, I would come to see how the quest to find the B-23 bomber was a lot like the quest we undertake when we seek the kingdom of God. Just like the wrong kind of bike will not enable you to complete your quest, so will the wrong philosophy thwart you in your pilgrimage toward the eternal destination God has planned for you. Only the right equipment (the gospel) can assure you get there. Giving in to the desires of the flesh (fatigue) can also derail your journey, and so can the obstacles (the giant boulders that caused Jim to crash) that the enemy places in our way. Others who have found the way (the quartet of bikers) can point you in the right direction, but you need to listen and respond to their words. The Holy Spirit can provide ways to sustain you in your quest (caffeine), even when you don't believe you can go any further. At some point you may find you need to let go of your attachment to material things (our mountain bikes) if you are to continue on in your journey. Then, at some point, you realize you need to enter the waters of baptism (crossing the stream), so that the understanding of death to your old self and the washing away of your sins are manifested viscerally. When you emerge, you begin to see the world differently than you ever saw it before (the image of Brian and Jim in the swamp), a vision of the real beauty of the world God intended for you to inhabit. At last you find the treasure (the B-23), which is Jesus Christ and the sacrifice He made for you on the cross so that you might have eternal life. There is no other treasure on earth that matches this, and no other adventure worth undertaking to get it.

PRIORITY

I finished updating "BMJ Emails" on my Mac and sent the document to my laptop so I could update it with any additional emails from my work account. Then I sent both the original and revised versions of "I Am Second" to Aaron, explaining the guiding principles behind the edits but leaving him the option of which one to use. Once I was back into my work email client I did a sort and saw that there were still quite a few emails that Brian and I had exchanged since 2009, so I spent the next couple of hours copying, pasting, and formatting the correspondences into "BMJ Emails." Re-reading these long-forgotten correspondences made Brian's life come alive again and, with it, the richness of our friendship. Besides planning many mountain-biking adventures, we had shared a lot of thoughts and experiences along the way, enough to number over a 1,000 email discussion threads.

I leaned back in the swivel chair at the writing desk and sighed deeply, staring blankly into space for the longest time as the parade of memories continued to wash over me until I realized that was it. Just like the missed opportunity to share the mountain-biking stories I'd written with Brian, there would be no more opportunities to make new memories of him in this lifetime. Feeling profoundly sad, I went back to work on my message, the sense of loss weighing heavily over me. After working the rest of the afternoon, I had still not completed the first draft, but decided to put it aside for the day and go visit Dena at the hospital.

Thursday morning came and since I'd only asked for Wednesday off, it was time to head back to the office. Yet, the more I went through the routine of getting ready to head out, the more unsettled I felt. Something wasn't right about the execution of my normal activities but I couldn't quite discern what the alternative course of action should be. Finally, as I stepped into the garage about to leave, I came to my senses and realized the futility of what I was doing. Even though my job was important, it was crazy to prioritize it over what God had purposed me to do at this specific time and place in life. Putting so much emphasis on work and success just so I would look good in the eyes of my boss and peers was a sick way to behave during a time like this. No doubt it was the core source of all the stress I felt, something I surely didn't need while trying to prepare the message for Brian's memorial service and work through the immediate effects of grief I was experiencing. It was obvious I was going down the wrong path, and the Holy Spirit was working to nudge me in another direction.

NUDGING

It was the Sunday after the Loon Lake treasure hunt and Brian and I were packing up his minivan to leave. Jim and Gary were driving straight back to Clarkston, but we were going to get another ride in before heading out of McCall. Earlier in the week, after studying the Payette National Forest map and scouring the internet, I had picked out a trail called the East Fork of Lake Fork Trail. It wasn't exactly a trail we could swing by on the way home, but the trailhead did not appear to be too far from Jim's cabin, and that was good enough.

Time was a big concern for me this Sunday morning. Not long after I committed to making the trip to McCall, I received a notice that someone whom I had grown very close to in the short time I knew him was getting ordained back in Spokane on the same weekend. His name was Brent Raska, although everyone called him Raska, as if that were an endearing nickname (and that's exactly what I thought it was when we first got introduced, unaware that it was his surname). Raska had interned as the director of youth ministries at the Congregational-Presbyterian church in Lewiston during the time I served on the board there, and we even got to do some mountain biking together. He had married the oldest daughter of some very dear friends of ours, Mark and Patti Benson. I taught Sunday School with Patti for several years while in Lewiston and worked for the same company Mark did up until 2008. Their oldest daughter was named Erin, and she would later become an ordained minister as well, but for now they were both about to head to Zambia on mission work after Raska's ordination on this very Sunday.

Word got around about the conflict I had and the logistical challenge I faced to make it back to the ceremony, and Debbie said that everyone she'd talked to about it said they would understand if I couldn't get there in time. Nevertheless, with all these close associations, plus the significance of the event, I felt the right thing to do was to make plans to attend. I had explained the situation to Brian and let him know of my intentions before we left Friday afternoon, but didn't talk about it too much beyond that.

At least that was the prevailing sentiment before I left for McCall that weekend. By Sunday morning the concept of making the ordination got a little more open ended. Instead of meaning the actual ceremony in the church, perhaps it meant just the reception afterwards. After all, that's when all the socializing would take place, and no one would see whether or not I was in the pew during the actual ceremony in the sanctuary of Whitworth Presbyterian Church on the north side of Spokane, about 45 minutes from home. Funny how a viewpoint can morph, a process no doubt influenced by the pinnacle riding experience to find the B-23, which left me hungry for more adventure.

We headed east on Lick Creek Road, bikes snugly snapped in on the top rack. I was going off memory on how to get to the trailhead, but I was beginning to regret not having a printout of the precise directions from the US Forest Service website. For some reason I was fixed on the notion that the trail was on the right side of the road, so for now I was peering out the passenger side window, looking for the cut through the land that indicated the location of the trail. I saw a warning sign for a weight-restricted bridge not too far ahead and right after that I saw a turnoff to a small camping area. That triggered a memory of a specific detail about the trailhead location: It was accessible from a campground.

"Right here," I stated with some urgency, hoping to slow Brian down to pull off before he sped past.

He braked hard and took the turn, then maneuvered the mini-van past the crude circle of stones around a blackened pit before killing the motor. We off-loaded our bikes and took off along the path heading north out of the clearing. We rode for about two minutes, and then the trail disappeared.

I dismounted my bike and took off through the brush, thinking I would see the trail re-emerge on the other side. Several downed trees lay ahead, their center sections a couple of feet off the ground. I stair-stepped my way up to the second tree and balanced on the fallen bole as I peered further into the brush until I concluded there was no more trail to follow. "Nope, dead end," I announced, turning around cautiously and heading back to where Brian waited. We rode back to the minivan, removed our gear, and re-fastened our bikes on top before resuming the journey on Lick Creek Road.

The misguided turn into the campground took at least twenty minutes out of our tight morning schedule. As luck would have it, we repeated the drill a second time when we came upon the Lake Fork Campground and concluded that was the place where the trailhead began, only to discover the trail unwinding on the other side of Lick Creek, which was too swollen to ford on foot. Another twenty minutes of precious time lost to a false start.

It was then that I remembered seeing the road sign warning of the weight-restricted bridge. Bingo! That was how we would get across the creek! So, once again we secured the bikes on top of the minivan and made one more jaunt further down the road and across the bridge. Shortly thereafter we came upon the entrance to the extended section of the Lake Fork Campground and the trailhead itself.

After gearing up a third time, we took off on the rocky path that was Lake Fork Trail. We hadn't ridden very far when I became aware of the thoughts swirling around in the background of my brain: I was harboring doubts as to whether I had made the right decision to disregard making the ordination. *Can I still make it?* I wondered.

I glanced at my watch and started doing some mental calculations to estimate how much longer we could ride and still allow time for me to make it back for the ceremony. Given the apparent steepness of the climb, I reckoned it would take us about twice as long to ascend Lake Fork Trail as it would to descend it. I already knew how long it took to get from McCall to my home in Spokane, and from there to the church, so I just had to approximate the time it would take to traverse Lick Creek Road back to McCall plus make a side stop in Lewiston to pick up my Xterra (I had left it at Brian's house so we could ride together in his van). I also had to estimate how long it would take for me to change clothes and freshen up before heading back out to the ceremony. After all these mental gyrations, I arrived at the conclusion that in order for me to make the ordination in time, we could ride up the trail for about thirty minutes.

Thirty minutes! It didn't seem fair! After all the trouble we'd been through to get here, plus the fact we only get to make weekend road trips to mountain-biking destination maybe once a year.

To heck with it, I thought. *We should at least get back the investment of time we've made into this ride already. Besides, it's a new trail in a new place. It's exploring. There's going to be excitement and adventure.*

But something kept pulling me back, kept telling me I needed to stick to the script about when to start heading back so I could make it in time to see Raska get ordained. I thought maybe I was getting concerned about avoiding a confrontation with Debbie, who would surely get mad at me for showing up late or missing his ordination altogether. *But that can't be right,* I reminded myself. We'd thoroughly discussed that possibility ahead of time, and she had said she was okay with that, since I had planned the bike ride before we got the invitation. Still, for whatever reason, the strenuousness of the climb could not distract me from this inner pull to return, but I kept cranking onward, following Brian up the steep and rocky trail through the forest.

We climbed some more, then the trail opened up into a clearing. *Now this is more like it!* I said to myself, excited to see some favorable change in the terrain. Just as the path before us beckoned our wheels to roll-on, I stole a quick glance at my watch. We'd reached the thirty-minute mark, the moment of truth between turning around to make it back to the ceremony in time or abandoning it altogether.

I clenched my jaw and started pedaling harder, thinking I'd made my decision. But contrary to my sudden physical resolve, I heard myself shout-out to Brian: "HOLD UP!"

Brian stopped right away and turned his bike around, watching as I pulled up alongside him. "What's wrong?" he asked.

"Look, if I'm going to get back to Spokane in time to make Raska's ordination, we have to turn around now. It's going to take us about fifteen minutes to get back to the car, another half hour to load the bikes and get back to McCall, three hours to Lewiston, fifteen minutes there to transfer my bike and gear to the Xterra, then two hours to Spokane, and another half hour for me to clean up, change clothes and get to Whitworth, which is another forty-five minutes from my house. We have to turn back now if I'm going to make it in time!"

I don't think Brian was expecting an engineering analysis at that moment, but if he had asked if we could just ride a little longer, or if I could just skip the ceremony and make the reception, I'm sure I would have capitulated. But he simply said, "All right," and while I felt bad about putting a quick end to the weekend and all the fun and adventure I knew he was having, my conscience felt good about what was starting to unfold.

The short ride back to the campground was thrilling in some spots and rough in others, and when it was over we rolled up to the Brian's van with smiles on our faces. We quickly packed away our gear, fastened the bikes on top, and then started the long journey home. Traffic was light on Idaho State Highway 55 as we left McCall. I figured we were getting a jump-start on the other weekenders heading back home as well which was good, because it meant unfettered travelling as we continued northward.

Being in a hurry, I was expecting the trip to seem like it was taking forever, but instead it went pretty fast, partly because Brian was doing his best to keep up the pace, but largely because of the gratification I got from spending time with a close friend and not wanting that to end. We talked about a lot of things on long trips such as this, but the conversations eventually distilled down to discussions of spiritual matters: where we were with our walk with the Lord, what were the temptations and struggles and set-backs we'd faced, and what were our hopes and longings for the future. In retrospect, I think the heart-to-heart exchanges like these are what really forged our friendship, perhaps more so than mountain biking.

We made it to Lewiston without incident, and I said a quick hello and goodbye to Dena, who handed me the keys to the Xterra after I'd loaded my bike into the rear cargo area. The egress from the one-way street on which Brian and Dena lived was always a little complicated, but I managed to get back on the main road out of town right in front of the local McDonald's. I was tired and hungry, so I turned into the drive-thru to order a large iced mocha and a Quarter Pounder, the fast-food sandwich whose sole virtue is that it's easy to eat while driving. As my car idled at the pick-up window waiting for my meal to arrive, I reached into the glove box and activated my iPod, configuring the setting to a random album mode for the drive home, leaving it up to God what music I listened to over the next two hours as I continued my way north on US 95.

A little over halfway home, "Good Monsters" by Jars of Clary started playing and continued playing for the remainder of my journey. As I approached the outskirts of Spokane, the opening measures of "Light Gives Heat" began, a musical critique of an overly Westernized approach to missions in Africa. The hauntingly ethereal voices of the African Children's Choir that accompanies the track made me think of Raska and Erin, who would soon be committing a year of their lives on that continent. There seemed to be a deep and meaningful synchronicity about the moment, and the song so moved me spiritually that I began to pray, asking God to empower Raska and Erin to do the work that is in his will in Zambia, and not their own.

"Light Gives Heat" ended, and the last song on the album started and played through just as I pulled into my driveway. I ran in, let the dogs out to do their business, stripped off by bike clothes directly into the laundry basket, slathered up with deodorant, put on some nice clothes, grabbed an energy drink for a caffeine boost (sound familiar?), corralled the dogs back inside and took off in the Xterra once again at 3:55, bike still in the back. I had to guess which would be the quickest route to take to get to Whitworth Presbyterian Church, as Raska's ceremony would be getting underway in just five minutes.

I arrived at 4:35, right in the middle of Tom Hanson's charge to Raska and Erin. Tom had been the associate pastor at the Congregational Presbyterian Church in Lewiston when Raska was there, and he was also a good friend to both Raska and Erin. I found Debbie, still thinking she was going to be mad at me for being late, but she just smiled at me and patted the empty spot next to her as if to say, "Here's the seat I saved for you."

Pastor Tom finished his message, and then, after a congregational hymn, all the active and former elders and deacons went to the front of the sanctuary to lay hands. I went and got a spot about two-deep behind Raska, but still managed to get my right hand on his shoulder. We were asked to lead off in prayer one at a time, as the spirit moved us. As others started to pray, my thoughts went back to "Light Gives Heat," and during a silent pause, the Spirit moved me to repeat the prayer I had offered on the drive home when I was listening to the song, but this time speaking it aloud. The prayer seemed to take on more significance when verbalized, as if I were speaking a blessing instead of a request. Once I finished, I realized that God had meant for me to be at the ceremony to impart those words, for whatever mysterious purpose and power he had behind them, and that he had indeed used the playlist on my iPod to prepare me for this moment. I was struck by a strong sense of peace and wonder realizing I had served His purpose, even if I didn't fully understand what was to become of it.

Returning to my seat, I thought about the turning point halfway up the mountain of Lake Fork Trail, when I wanted to go on, but I knew I would disappoint someone if I didn't go, thinking that someone would be Debbie. As it turned out, I realized the real object of that disappointment would have been the Holy Spirit. Thank God he got through to me—and Brian too, since he agreed to turn around without any sign of anger or remorse.

In retrospect, I can now see the many other times I've experienced that strong nudge like I did on the mountain that day. That one pointed me to a foreknown event, but most of them just point me to do something I hadn't planned to do. In a sense, they are like those pop-up reminders you get on your phone or computer for upcoming calendar appointments, except they are not on your calendar, but on God's calendar, and He's trying to get your attention to attend to them. When I respond in obedience, I quickly discover that He leads me somewhere to do his work, usually to minister to somebody. It's such an exciting and delightful and humbling surprise to be used like that, and I regret all the times I've shrugged off those nudges because I've been too busy with my own agenda. If there is such a thing as a sacrament of the moment, where every instant is an opportunity to execute God's will, then I want to continually partake of it. Let the nudges continue, and pray that I'm ever responsive to each and every one of them.

PROGRESS

August 7, 2014

I responded to the strong nudge in the garage by heading back into the house and emailing my boss again, relaying that I needed more time off today and would take Friday off as well. But I had to compromise some, since there were two deadlines looming that week that no one else was equipped to handle that quickly. I committed to getting both of those done by that afternoon.

I changed out of my work clothes and headed back to the trail in the woods next to my house, again taking with me a sheet of paper and a pen. Not far from the quiet place where I had been praying stood a tree and a stump side by side, providing a perfect spot to sit down and lean back. As I quieted down I realized just how much sorrow was still in my heart, so I started pouring it out to God in prayer, only to think about how much more sadness Dena and the girls must be feeling, and then remembering Jeremy's situation as well, as he had to be experiencing the loss at least at the same intensity as I was. I asked God to bring comfort to us all, then the last thing I prayed was for help in fulfilling the three objectives that had been set before me. When I had finished I sat still and waited for a response. I remained there for a long time until I was moved to head back home.

The inspiration came much more quickly this time, scarcely a minute after I'd gotten up to leave. I started recalling all kinds of specific episodes in Brian's life that demonstrated his character and I filled up the paper with just enough notes to help me remember what I needed to write about. When I got back to the house, I moved my work area from the study to the dining room table so I could spread out more. I was able to flesh out more details from the email records I had compiled, supplemented with some information I got by reaching out to Dena plus a couple of Brian's friends and acquaintances. I was making progress thanks to God's faithfulness in responding to my prayers.

My work commitments detoured me for four hours that afternoon, and I resumed working on Brian's message around dinnertime, pausing long enough to savor some smoked salmon dressed with fresh lime and dill that a friend from church had prepared and brought over for Debbie and I to eat. I was touched by his act of kindness, and it encouraged me to dig in to complete the first draft. By ten o'clock that evening it was finished, but I was mentally exhausted. Zack was on his way from Seattle, but I did not think I could to wait up for him much longer. He'd been delayed on the mountain pass due to some road construction work that required blasting and wouldn't get in until well after midnight. I left the front door unlocked for him and went to bed, finding sleep quickly.

ASHES

August 8, 2014

I woke up early Friday morning. After making coffee I jumped into the Word before heading back out to the woods to pray. The trail had become a sanctuary for me, a wilderness substitute where I could bare my soul to God and experience His comfort and peace.

I cooked some breakfast when I got back, then checked my text messages. Birdsell notified me that Brian's ashes and death certificates were ready to pick up. He'd asked me Tuesday if I could get them, thinking that by the time they would be ready, Ashley would be checked out of the hospital and he, along with everybody else, would be back in Lewiston. Turned out Ashley was getting released that morning, yet he was going to be too tied up to run out to the Spokane Valley from downtown to get them, so I let him know I'd still take care of it.

I sat down at the dining room table and opened up the first draft of the message for Brian's service and worked on it until eleven thirty. Zack was just then getting out of bed, having slept in on account of his late arrival home. I saved my work and asked him to go with me to pick up Brian's ashes. Given he hadn't eaten since six o'clock the night before, I told him we could stop at his favorite fast food joint along the way, an incentive that pretty much guaranteed he would accompany me.

Just as we were leaving, a text came in from Aaron asking me to give him a call so he could pray over me right before I went in to pick up Brian's remains. I let him know I would. I was beginning to realize that Aaron was a bold and unabashed prayer warrior, a tremendous encouragement during times like these and a quality that you only see in men of strong faith.

It was about twelve thirty when Zack and I pulled into the parking lot of the crematorium located on one of the busiest streets in the city of Spokane Valley. I called Aaron and put him on speaker, and when he started to pray I had to roll up the windows and turn off the ignition since the din of the nearby traffic and the noise from the air conditioning kept us from hearing him. The temperature was in the mid-eighties outside, and the Xterra's interior quickly became unbearably hot. Sweat beads formed on the end of my nose and dripped into my lap, but Zack and I did our best to continue praying along with Aaron as we sweltered in what now felt like a mini-furnace. It seemed ironic that we were being exposed to such intense heat in front of a crematorium.

When Aaron said "Amen" I hastened to hang up so I could fire up the engine again to get the air conditioner blasting. Zack waited in the car while I went inside the crematorium and spoke with a woman who was sitting in an office, telling her I was there to pick up Brian's remains and his death certificates. Since Birdsell had paved the way for me to be there, it did not take long for her to retrieve a box from a back room. Then she pulled out a large envelope from a filing drawer and handed both to me. I thanked her and left.

The box felt like it weighed about thirty pounds and was wrapped in the kind of paper you might expect to find on an off-year anniversary gift—patterned, but not ostentatious. Brian had been a tall man and a very lean and strong 185 pounds, and the cognitive dissonance of thinking how that physicality had been reduced to the contents of this box about the size of a cubic foot was bewildering. It didn't seem real, but I could not deny the reality that the body is just the temporary house for our soul and the remaining elements of his earthly existence were now my responsibility.

Zack and I headed back home so we could start packing for the trip to Lewiston. I parked in the garage, but hesitated before getting out of the Xterra. It didn't seem right to leave Brian's remains in the backseat while I was inside getting ready. He deserved something more dignified than being treated like a package in a delivery truck, so I took the box with me. Once inside the house, though, I faced the dilemma of where to put it. Now that Brian was at rest, maybe it made sense to put him in the bedroom where he and Dena had always slept whenever Debbie and I hosted them and the girls on their weekend trips to Spokane. I climbed the stairs and delicately placed the box next to the pillow on the bed, then went back downstairs and started packing.

While I was rummaging through my clothes trying to decide what to wear for the memorial service, Debbie came home with a friend who was visiting from Oregon. They had not been home when I pulled in, as she had met her friend at the bottom of the hill leading to our sub-division, since the directions to our house can be somewhat confusing to the first time visitor. I stepped out of our downstairs bedroom to say hello, and then retreated back to the closet to resume packing. I emerged a few minutes later to retrieve something from the dining room only to see Debbie upstairs giving her friend a tour of the house. The next room she was going to show was the bedroom where she would be sleeping that night, which happened to be the same bedroom where I had placed Brian's ashes, which neither one of them knew anything about.

Oh no, now what do I do? I thought. I was about to shout, *Don't go in there!*, but what would I say if they asked why? I couldn't lie, but how could I explain that my best friend's physical remains were on the very same bed that Debbie's friend would be sleeping on that night? Would it put her in a socially awkward position where she wouldn't want to say anything but feel really bothered about having to stay in the room? Would it mortify Debbie to the point where she would have to find some way to compensate for the arrangements? I didn't know, nor did I know what to do next, and it was at that point that I realized I simply had to surrender the moment to God, and let him take care of it. I prayed silently as the two of them walked into the bedroom.

SURRENDER

The day was starting to get warm—*really* warm—as if the heat were building into a weightiness that would press the dust in the air back into the ground. It was a Saturday morning in July 2004, around ten o'clock, and Brian and I were done with mountain biking for the day. After three hours of hard riding, we now stood at the Four Corners intersection atop Moscow Mountain, waiting for the MAMBA crew to show up. MAMBA was short for Moscow Area Mountain Biking Association, one of the most dedicated groups of trail builders I'd ever seen. As much enjoyment as Brian and I took from riding on Moscow Mountain, we figured it was only right to give something back. So, from time to time we would volunteer to help with MAMBA's "trail parties," the term they coined for getting a bunch of volunteers together to build or maintain the trails on the mountain. Unknown to me at that time, my trail building efforts on this day would have repercussions some seven years later.

Four Corners gets a lot of sun exposure, so Brian and I moved our bikes over to a patch of shade near the edge of the woods and continued waiting. In the distance we could hear the whining sound of an engine in low gear. Before long a truck came into sight. It pulled over and stopped next to the blue gate blocking access to the west side of the ridge road that ran along the top of the mountain. Right away another truck appeared and pulled in behind it. I recognized the driver who climbed out of the first truck: It was Jim LaFortune, and I went over to shake his hand.

I first met Jim through the pages of a book he wrote called, *Mountain Bike Guide to Hog Heaven*. Back in 1996, a friend who had gone to the University of Idaho introduced me to mountain biking on Moscow Mountain. This was back in the days of dial-up modems for accessing the internet, which still wasn't quite the repository of information like it is today, where you can join MAMBA and get on-line access to the more than three dozen trails on the mountain. Jim's narrow, spiral-bound booklet was the only way to locate and navigate the dozen or so trails that were known on the mountain at that time. Jim was more than just the founder of MAMBA—he was a steady source of inspiration and motivation to the MAMBA members in their trail building efforts.

Then Brian and I introduced ourselves to the second driver, Dan Cordon. In the summer of 2004, Dan was in the process of becoming a co-leader of MAMBA, as Jim was preparing to take on another role within the club. Dan already displayed admirable leadership traits as the energetic organizer of the trail parties and other club events, as well as a prolific and humorous chronicler of all their activities.

"Okay, everyone," Dan shouted. "Grab some tools and let's head over to Cave Trail."

"Wow! Look at all this cool equipment," Brian said as he surveyed the items in Jim and Dan's truck beds.

Sure enough, it was quite the collection of trail building tools: Pulaskis (a two-sided tool with an axe on one end and a hoe on the other), digging shovels, MacLeods (another two-sided tool with a coarse rake and a flat blade), grub hoes, fire rakes, pick axes, "Sith blades" (somehow the brush saws got that nickname, probably from a bored trail builder acting out his Star Wars fantasies), chain saws, loppers, pole saws, and weed whips. Brian and I each grabbed as much as we could carry and followed Jim and Dan across Four Corners to the yet-developed trailhead for Cave Trail.

After passing through some brush, we came upon some recently built track and followed it until we hit a series of small, regularly spaced flags that plotted out the rest of the course that the volunteers would build. At that point Dan divided us up into smaller groups and had us spread out along the trail line. As Brian and I hiked over to the section we would be responsible for, we passed a small cave that gave rise to the trail's name. Dan assigned Brian and me to a section on a steep slope just beyond the cave.

"We'd better make sure we're careful where we put our stuff," I remarked. "If something were to get away from us and start rolling down the hill, I'd hate to have to go way down there to retrieve it."

"Sounds good," Brian agreed. "Let's get to work."

We each picked up a Pulaski and set to it. After a couple of hours Jim came around and suggested everyone break for lunch. Brian and I climbed up the side of the mountain to a shaded area with lots of large, flat rocks, perfect for sitting and stretching out. We ate peanut butter and jelly sandwiches, nuts, and some protein bars, washing it down with water from our CamelBaks. I had found a spot on the rocks next to Jim, and we started talking. At one point the subject of travel came up.

"Where have you been?" I asked, after naming some of the countries I'd had to travel to for work.

"I was in the Peace Corps in the seventies in Paraguay," Jim began, his voice sounding a little distant.

"Really?" I exclaimed excitedly, seeing that we had something in common. "I was there last year visiting the exchange student our family hosted back in 2000. He lives in Asuncion."

"I was in Ciudad del Este," Jim replied.

My excitement picked up. "Our exchange student's dad had to go there on business so he took us along," I said. "We spent some time downtown while he worked, and afterwards he took us to Iguaçu Falls." Jim was silent, so I continued talking. "To be honest, parts of Ciudad del Este seemed more third world than developed. In fact, it felt a little menacing at times."

"I didn't have a good experience there," Jim began. "I was mugged one night while walking down a deserted street. They took my valuables and then they stabbed me and left me there to bleed to death. Fortunately someone found me and got me to a hospital. I was there a long time until I finally made enough of a recovery to return to the States."

"Oh, no," I murmured, my voice stifled by the horror of what I just heard.

"See these?" Jim asked, pointing to several scars on his face. "That's some of the remnants of the damage they did."

As I leaned in for a closer examination, I thought I also saw some indications of slight deformities protruding upward through his skin, perhaps where parts of his skull had been broken in the attack, but I wasn't sure. Then a distressing change descended over Jim and, in a brief moment, I caught a glimpse of the suffering that he had endured, as if the anguished memory of the event had resurfaced just long enough to reconfigure his countenance and expose the loneliness and terror of being assaulted like that in such a strange and ruthless city. Even though it was only a momentary glance into the trauma of his past, it troubled me immensely. "That had to have been a frightening time in your life."

"It was," Jim said. Then his buoyant spirit rebounded and his voice returned to normal. "But life is good now. Just look at all the good work we're doing here today and think about how much we're going to enjoy riding on another new trail."

"Yeah," I nodded, glad to see Jim shaking off the terrible memory. For a moment, I reflected on all the fun adventures Brian and I had experienced on the mountain, and how the experiences seemed to always draw us closer to God. That led me to admit, "It is good."

We talked a little longer until we finished lunch. By then I was thoroughly impressed with the ease that Jim had deployed in making me feel like a longtime friend, even though we had never really talked that much before. Unbeknownst to me at the time, that was to be the last opportunity I'd ever get to know Jim personally. Five years later Jim would confront a fiend worse than the one he encountered in Ciudad del Este. A brain tumor mugged his vitality at the high point of his life, and after a brave and dignified struggle he succumbed, leaving behind a wife and two children. Jim LaFortune's legacy is written all over Moscow Mountain, and on that hot Saturday on July I was blessed to have been able to break bread with him.

After lunch, work got a little more challenging for Brian and me. The soil was loose on the more exposed sections and in some spots it just crumbled away and tumbled down the steep hill every time we tried to make a level cut into the slope. One way to fix that was to ram a log lengthwise into the bank just below the trail line. The log would dam up the collapsing dirt, which we could then tamp down to form a smooth path to ride over. We also discovered another technique for doing this where some clever builders had simply bent over a juvenile hardwood tree growing next to the trail and embedded it into the soil to provide a buttress to hold the dirt in place.

The first two times where we needed to reinforce the trail, I hiked up the hill into the woods to find an appropriately sized log to do the trick. On the third instance we noticed a juvenile hardwood growing next to where the marker flags indicated the trail needed to be. The sapling was limbless and leafless and looked like it could have come from a cottonwood sucker. To my surprise, as I bent it down to see if it would make adequate reinforcement, it stayed bent down, as if the trunk had atrophied to a collection of pliant but inelastic fibers. We buried the tip of the tree into the hillside and placed a large rock on top of it just to be sure it stayed down. Then we leveled out the cut along the length of the bole and packed in the dirt.

Shortly after that Dan Cordon came by. "Hey, Brian, Ike. How's it going?"

"Good," we answered in unison, halting our work for the moment.

"Just want to let you know we'll be wrapping up the trail party in about an hour and a half. So, plan accordingly." He looked around as we acknowledged, then added. "This is some nice work, guys."

Fishing for more praise, I pointed to the section where we utilized the cottonwood sapling to support the trail. "Look at how we were able to use a tree growing next to the trail," I said.

Dan walked over the recently completed section and nodded his head up and down. He complemented us, saying, "Now that's a creative use of the surrounding environment. Well done."

I beamed, probably more than Brian, who was never the type of person to seek praise from others, but I'm sure he was just as encouraged by Dan's words as I was. "Thanks, Dan," I acknowledged for both of us.

We set back to work with renewed vigor to finish as much of the hillside as we could before it came time to quit. In wasn't long after that when we started chopping into another section of hillside only to once again see the cut disintegrate into loose dirt and trickle down the steep hillside. As luck would have it, another sapling was growing next to the area marked for the new trail. "Let's use this tree to support the trail," I said to Brian, still savoring the gratification I took from the way we'd utilized the last sapling.

"Okay," he replied, and stopped his work to watch.

I grabbed the sapling and pushed on it, bending it down toward the ground, expecting it to lie perfectly horizontal on the hillside so Brian could commence shoveling dirt against it. Instead, it wavered back up—not completely, but about three-fourths of the way upright. So I pushed it down again, and this time it rose up about two-thirds of the way. At least I was making progress.

Down again I pushed, and this time the sapling recovered halfway to its originally vertical position. This seemed to be the best I could get, as subsequent pushes kept bringing it back to this same orientation. Brian jumped in and tamped a big pile of dirt on the top end of the sapling while I held it down. We backed away and then waited for a moment until we were satisfied that it was going to hold. We started filling dirt into the spaces along the bole, and just as we were about to finish, the young tree rose like a feeble spirit called-up from the grave, and all the dirt we had packed spilled away.

Probably sensing futility before I could, Brian moved onward, making cuts along the rest of the trail markers while I continued working with the uncooperative tree. I buried it again, using more dirt and fiercer stomping to tamp it down, and it appeared to have worked. I hurried to fill in the reinforcing dirt along the bole, then flattened out the path before heading along to catch up with Brian. It held for about five minutes then popped up.

I went back and tried again, and again after that, and then even twice more after that. Brian took note of my obsessive behavior and came back to help. I found a rock and put on top of the buried tip, but the rock rolled down the hill, so I went and found a flatter one. It stayed in place, and the sapling stayed down, and we quickly filled in the rest of the dirt, but some mysterious force unearthed the tip around the edge of the rock and the tree rose again, displacing all the dirt we'd laid.

I went at it again, bashing the tip into the ground with the rock in near-frenzied motions, then burying the tip under as much dirt as I could scoop up. Still, it wouldn't hold. I became oblivious to what was happening around me, and failed to notice that Brian had picked up a saw and climbed the hill to saw off a piece of fallen timber which provided the right length we needed to reinforce that section. When he returned, he stood quietly next to me and said, "Let's use this."

I stopped, looked at Brian, and then looked at the pathetic-looking sapling. Why wouldn't it stay down like the first one? It was such a perfect solution…utilizing the existing environment to build the trail. I wanted to keep trying, but I could sense some undercurrent within me saying to stop trying so hard. *Let it go…surrender.*

Sighing, I took the other end of the piece of timber Brian held and we fitted it into the hillside. The dirt packed very nicely under it, and the log and everything else stayed in place. We moved along, finishing as much of the assigned trail section as we could before we had to call it a day. Although that was our last contribution to trail building that year, work continued on the Cave Trail through the rest of the summer and into the fall, when the trail was completed.

After seasoning over winter, the Cave Trail was ready to ride in late spring when all the snow had melted. Brian and I were eager to ride it and made it a priority on our first visit onto the mountain in 2005. "Here comes the section we built last year," I shouted to Brian as we'd passed the cave and approached the first tree that we had bent over successfully. It was still in the ground and still doing its job. Then I sighted the sapling that I had tried in vain to use in the same fashion. Remarkably, it had just about completely uprighted itself, despite all the damage I had inflicted on it last year trying to make it stay down. The cave and those two trees would be landmarks identifying "our" section of the trail from that day forward, and over the next six years, the downed tree continued to stay down, and the sapling continued to grow, becoming bigger and sturdier as the seasons passed.

Fall of 2011 arrived, and the two-hour separation between Brian and me had gotten in the way of having a good spring and summer season of mountain biking together. But there was a hint of redemption in the air on a cold and wet morning toward the end of September when Brian and I hit Moscow Mountain for what would probably be our last ride together for the season. I drove down from Spokane, and Brian drove up from Lewiston, and we met about a half-hour before sunrise on Warnick Road, a dead-end spur that angles off the main Moscow Mountain Road, which traverses the mountain from Moscow to Troy.

The damp and chilly air clung to us like a blanket soaked in liquid nitrogen, making us eager to get moving so we could shake off the cold. We carried our bikes across a log bridge which deposited us on the downhill end of Cabin Trail and began the long crank upward, using the network of trails and the main road to reach our intended starting point, Nemesis Trail, about 800 feet higher in elevation than where we started. Brian gestured for me to take the lead on the Nemesis descent, and I accepted, knowing that I would have to really push it to keep from holding him up. I took off fast, before he had clipped in, knowing that if I built up enough distance between us at the start, I could keep ahead of him.

It was exhilarating. Nemesis is one of those technical trails full of switchbacks and sudden, steep rises, but if you ride it enough, you can figure out how to do it without stalling or having to dismount—you know, have one of those perfect rides and that was the experience for us that morning. I exited the end of Nemesis, heart pumping full of excitement, and we crossed the main road to the start of the Lickety Split trail, where I told Brian it was his turn to lead. On and on we went, taking turns on each successive juncture that we came to, until it was my turn to lead on the next trail in the sequence: Cave Trail.

It was my first time on Cave Trail in well over a year. We rode it a lot the first few years after we helped build it, but then started backing off. Cave Trail was very technical, and it drops you in a hole that required a lot of steep cranking to get out of. We never talked about it, but I think we both came to the conclusion it just wasn't as much fun as some of other trails to ride on the mountain, especially when time was a limiting factor.

But today was different. I attacked Cave Trail hard, finding a flow and speed I'd never experienced before on the trail. We descended through the trees, then across a draw and along the mountain, then at length arriving at the narrow plank of wood that crossed over the rut caused by the water that ran out from the cave during the wet seasons. Seeing the cave told me that our section was soon coming up, and sure enough we found ourselves cruising along the steep, sandy bank with the scarcity of vegetation on its side. I started pedaling hard, eager to really stretch out the speed as much as possible, since the trail had become relatively flat.

I was looking ahead for the familiar landmarks. There was the first one—the downed tree, still holding up (or down) after all these years. I increased the cadence to pick up some more speed, knowing the final descent down the steep hill was coming up soon.

The way I was handling the bike to pump up more speed made it act like a wigwag signal at a railroad stop. Left and right it rocked, until I got too close to the upside of the bank with my right pedal, which interrupted my rhythm with a jolt and sent the front wheel wobbling. I was losing control quickly, gyrating toward the cottonwood tree that I had worked so hard to pound into the dirt seven years earlier. Just then, the front wheel went over the edge of the bank and the bike started plunging. I jumped off and grabbed the tree as the bike came out from under me and plummeted down the steep bank until it folded up into itself in a crash at the bottom. I had spun around the tree and landed back on the trail, feet firmly on the ground.

"Wow!" Brian shouted. He had been close enough behind me to see every bit of the near catastrophe unfold.

"This tree saved my life!" I exclaimed, my hands still gripping against the bole, as if they were welded to it.

Only God knows what would have happened to me had that tree not been there. I'm sure I would not have escaped as painlessly as I did that morning. I'm convinced God knew when Brian and I were building the trail that it would be good for my sake to have that little tree stay upright when I was so desperately trying to keep it down. I also think he had put Brian as his mediating agent to silently persuade me to give it up, although Brian—like me—could not have imagined that was going on at the time. I am so grateful I listened to that tiny voice—the Spirit of God intersecting with my thoughts, guiding me to keep me safe—telling me to let go, to surrender.

God knows better than me, always, every time. His Spirit is relentless in its pursuit to penetrate my consciousness and get my attention so it can show me the path I should take for His glory and for the best He has in store for me. If only I were to surrender everything— and I mean everything—to His will, would I always be in His paths, always choosing the things that bring life instead of destruction. Fortunately, that early fall morning on Moscow Mountain I stayed on the path because of the act of surrendering seven years earlier.

THE LAST ROAD TRIP

August 8, 2014

I continued to pray silently as Debbie and her friend walked into the bedroom where Brian's remains sat nicely packaged on top of the bed spread. They lingered there for a few moments, chatted, and then walked out to view the next room on the tour. I waited for what I thought was the inevitable question: *Ike? What's that box on the bed for?* But none came, making me wonder if God had answered my prayer by making them temporarily blind to the obvious.

Whew, I thought to myself. *That was close. Thank you, Lord.* Maybe it was just a release from the tension, but I giggled. In an unexpected way, God had provided a comical moment in the midst of all the grief I was experiencing that week. I thought to myself, *This is the kind of thing Brian would find funny, too.*

Shortly after that, Zack and I finished packing so we loaded our gear into the Xterra. Before shutting down my laptop, I printed out the current draft of the message I was going to deliver at his memorial service. Then I slipped back into the upstairs bedroom unnoticed and retrieved the box with Brian's ashes, returning them to the back seat of the Xterra. We took off into a beautiful, sunny afternoon.

I thought it fitting that we should drive down to Lewiston on the slightly longer route through Idaho so we could take Brian's remains past Moscow Mountain one last time. As the familiar contours of the mountain came into view, I couldn't help but think of all the hours we'd spent up there in fellowship and fun, and how mountain biking had forged a friendship like nothing short of the one that David and Jonathan shared nearly 3,000 years earlier. My eyes welled up with tears: so much past joy, so much present sadness. I stared at the mountain as long as I could, realizing all I had now were memories, that Brian would ride with me no more save for the remainder of this last road trip.

We arrived in Lewiston at around half past three and swung by the paper mill complex where Brian worked so I could tend to a request that Dena had asked me to help her with that involved the mill's human resources department. Then we went straight to the Nazarene Church, where I greeted Jeremy and asked how he was doing. He and some other men of the church were working to set up the giant canvas awning for the outdoor barbecue planned for after the service, so Zack and I pitched in to help. Then we caught a ride with Jeremy to join many of the volunteers for a group dinner over at a local pizza joint. There were about thirty of us in all, and Jeremy and I split the bill on our credit cards, but everyone chipped in afterwards to cover the cost.

After dinner, Jeremy took us back to the church where I transferred Brian's ashes over to him. Leaving them in the Xterra at the church did not seem like a big deal like it had been earlier when I didn't want to leave them in my garage, since church was a place where Brian truly enjoyed being. The three of us prayed, then Zack and I said goodbye to Jeremy and headed up to Ryan Skinner's house, where we were staying for the night.

Ryan Skinner was a former gridiron great at the University of Idaho in the late 1990s, back during the time they beat the odds to become the Big West champions and upset Southern Miss to win the Humanitarian Bowl. Since then, Ryan had hung up his football cleats for golf, mountain biking, and snowboarding. I met him through a co-worker back in the early 2000s when I was searching for a financial advisor. Our shared interest in mountain biking had led us to start riding together some, which is how he met Brian. One thing led to another, and he eventually became Brian's financial advisor, too. It was a good thing, as he had been responsible for making sure that Dena would be very well taken care of in case something ever happened to Brian.

Ryan and his family were out when we got to his home, but he had left us instructions on where to find the key. After getting in, Zack and I helped ourselves to the refrigerator, then made our way downstairs to Ryan's man-cave where we relaxed for a while before going to bed. We were sound asleep by the time Ryan and his family returned home, and we didn't hear them come in.

AN ANOINTING

I woke up early the next morning, read some in the Bible and prayed, then looked at yesterday's printout of the message I'd prepared. I began to see areas where I could improve on it so I started marking it up with a pen. Pretty soon there were so many marks and margin notes that it became difficult to follow. By then, Ryan was up and had made us some coffee, so I asked him if I could update the manuscript on his personal computer. He booted it up while I forwarded the latest draft of the message to him from the "Sent" folder on my iPhone, which was synchronized with the email client on my work computer. Ryan opened up his email and downloaded the draft onto the desktop of his computer, where I began typing in the latest round of edits from the notes I had scribbled on the printout.

When I had finished and had hit the print button, the black ink cartridge was so low that it ran out before the first page of the message could eject from the printer. I fetched Ryan for help and he started rummaging through the drawers at his workstation, trying to find a spare cartridge, but there were none. It seemed like the enemy was trying to frustrate the delivery of my message again! I asked Ryan if we could email the revised version to his work office and print it out there, but that would have made me late for when I was supposed to show up at the church, and it would have put Ryan way behind in getting ready for attending the service, too.

I prayed for wisdom on what to do, then went back to the revised version and selected all the text, and changed the font to the darkest color on the palette that didn't use black. Turns out that was purple, which printed fine and presented no readability problems when viewed from the distance of reading from a lectern. In a sense, it was a better solution than black, since it reminded me of the liturgical color for Easter, symbolic of Christ's royalty. This reaffirmed my experience that God is always quick and faithful to answer our prayers for wisdom when we ask.

Zack was going to catch a ride to the church with Ryan, so I took off alone and got there just as some ushers were finishing setting up seats in the overflow area to the north of the main stage of the worship center. I met the head pastor of the church, Cliff Purcell, who was helping set up the stage for the service. Brian's mountain bike, kayak, backcountry skis, motorcycle and other artifacts of his active outdoor life style adorned the stage, along with a large picture of him with his family taken at one of the beaches on the Oregon coast. Cliff instructed me to head downstairs to the church office where he and the rest of the speakers that morning would be assembling before the service.

I ran into Debbie on the way, as she had just arrived from Spokane. I told her I had to go meet with Cliff but that there were some seats set aside for us on the front row in the worship center. She said she'd meet me there, but for the time being she would go and visit with some old friends she'd sighted on her way into the building. I eventually made it to the church office and took a seat against a bookcase as one by one the rest of Brian's closest friends filled the room: Jeremy Carr, Aaron Middleton, Dan LejaMeyer, Todd Johnson and Gary Grabow. Gary worked for the same company that Brian and I worked for and had mountain biked with us in the past. In fact, long before Carl Strong joined Brian and me for the adventurous weekend in the McCall area that climaxed at the Tamarack Resort, he had first ridden with Gary, Brian, and me on Moscow Mountain. It was a fun but fateful trip, as Gary wrecked and broke his collarbone that day, but Carl knew first aid well enough to attend to him until he could get to the emergency room at the local hospital.

Now that all the speakers were assembled around the walls of the church office, Cliff explained that he was going to anoint us with oil to ensure the presence and protection of the Holy Spirit during our time speaking on stage. I had never before received an anointing, and a deep sense of reverence descended on me as the quiet rite unfolded. As his thumb pressed the oil against my forehead, Cliff spoke a blessing over me, and it reminded me of the first anointing of the Holy Spirit that I received when I became a child of God by accepting Jesus Christ as my Lord and Savior. When Cliff had finished, I became filled with a sense of peace and calm very much like what I'd experienced at the moment of my salvation. In retrospect, I realize there haven't been many times since then where God had seen it fit to remind me viscerally that He was now always with me. This anointing was one of them, and it made me think of one other time—apart from the time I became a Christian—when I'd experienced that mysterious but tangible reassurance of His eternal presence.

BAPTISM

Mountain biking was in its infancy in 1989, a time when the sport offered nothing more to ride on than durable frames with fat, knobby tires. My first mountain-bike ride was during those early years of the sport. I was attending a corporate retreat in Durango, Colorado, and one afternoon I slipped away to rent a bike from the local bike shop and take a ride on a steep dirt road called "Horse Gulch." I was hooked after that one ride, but after returning home to Mississippi (where I lived at the time), I had to content myself with other outdoor activities, since mountain biking in the Magnolia State was unheard of. Of course, that would change for the better when I moved to the Pacific Northwest.

Nevertheless, part of the allure of mountain biking is closely tied to my fondness in general of engaging in physical activity outdoors. So when I received an invitation to undertake a weeklong expedition into the Boundary Waters Canoe Wilderness Area in Northern Minnesota, I couldn't turn it down. Jerome Herro was the organizer of the trip. I met Jerome when I was attending graduate school in Appleton, Wisconsin and we got to be close friends. He was in the class behind me and was also a teammate of mine with the Appleton Rugby Club. He'd called me one afternoon when I was working my job at a paper mill in Alabama.

"Hey, I'm planning a trip to the Boundary Waters with a couple of buddies of mine. Do you want to go?" His distinctively Wisconsin tone of voice stood in stark contrast to all the southern accents that surrounded me in my day-to-day interactions at the mill.

"Where are the Boundary Waters?" I asked. "I've never heard of them."

"You've never heard of the Boundary Waters?" he scoffed. "It's only the greatest fishing spot in the entire world!"

I was intrigued. "Tell me more," I said.

"Get a map and look at the border between Minnesota and Canada," Jerome commanded. "There're over a thousand lakes there, which means there're tons of fish there, too."

"So, it's a fishing expedition, right?"

"Yep," he confirmed. "And I got everything we'll need for the trip. Canoes, tents, camping gear, food, even a fishing pole if you don't have one."

"I don't," I confessed, "but maybe my brother-in-law who lives near Appleton has one that I can borrow."

"So do you think you can go?" Jerome asked, sounding optimistic that I would accept.

"Yeah, I'd love to. I could use a break from all this stress at the mill. I need to talk to Debbie first to see if she's okay with me leaving her alone with the kids for a week."

"All right, let me know how that turns out, " Jerome said.

That evening I told Debbie about Jerome's call, gingerly releasing the details of his invitation so I had time to discern if she would get ruffled at my audacity for wanting to disappear from the family for a whole week. I guess it must have been very apparent to her that I really did need to get away from work, as she was very gracious about consenting to let me go. So, I made the necessary travel arrangements and before long found myself flying off to Wisconsin on a Friday afternoon and arriving late that night. Debbie's brother picked me up at the Appleton airport and took me to his bachelor pad in Larson. As an avid outdoorsman, he was more than eager to see his normally non-hunting, non-fishing brother-in-law take up some of the more manly accouterments of the outdoor life, so the next day he equipped me with a fishing rod and a tackle box and loaned me his camouflage pants, jacket and hat, all made out of Gore-Tex.

I caught up with Jerome later that afternoon at his home in Kimberly. We packed his station wagon with the camping equipment and fastened two canoes to the top. We then made a trip to the sporting goods store, where he helped me select the right kind of lures I would need to successfully attract pikes and walleyes. That evening, after being treated to the last home-cooked meal we would have for over a week, we settled in for some brews and reminiscences of our rugby days before hitting the sack. Early the next morning his two former high-school buddies, Bill and Jeff, met us at Jerome's house and we transferred their gear into Jerome's station wagon before taking off for the 480-mile journey.

It was a long trip, and it wasn't until mid-afternoon that we pulled off the highway onto Gunflint Trail, the main access road to the Boundary Waters. The weather was sunny and warm, and I had the window down, tapping my hand against the body of the car to the rhythm of Creedence Clearwater Revival's "Keep on Chooglin'." The music's beat propelled us along the dirt road to our destination: a turn-off to an empty parking lot next to the shore of Round Lake, our put-in point.

"That's the last time we'll have wheels under us for the next six days," Jerome informed us as we got out of the car.

We unloaded the gear and packed the canoes. Since I was the inexperienced canoeist, Jerome told me to take the seat in the bow and said he would instruct me on what to do from there. As we pushed off into the water, I could feel my heart pounding in my eardrums. I was excited about beginning a brand new adventure, but also a little anxious about not screwing up with the paddle. A conditioned response, I suppose, telling me that I really did need that break from work, where mistakes brought the immediate wrath of managers responsible for production goals.

Civilization disappeared behind us as we pulled through the still waters, Jerome and I leading the way, and Bill and Jeff following behind us. It wasn't long before we made landfall on the southwest corner of Round Lake, Jerome doing a good job of finding the portage spot just by comparing the lay of the land to the map. We got out of the canoes and I got my first lesson in portaging. First of all, the trail length to the next lake was given in rods, a unit of measure I'd come across in the King James Version of the Bible, but had no idea what a rod meant in terms of feet or miles. Next, there was the challenge on how to carry the canoes and gear over that distance. In all, it was quite a hefty load, as lightweight canoes manufactured with space-age materials were not very common back in the late 1980s.

I snatched the canoe overhead and held it aloft with outstretched arms, as if I were in the gym doing an overhead press with a pair of dumbbells. It was a bit fatiguing, but the portage wasn't long and I was able to make it without having to set the canoe back on the ground. The second portage, however, was something different. This portage would take us to Tuscarora Lake, 366 rods away. Not knowing this was a little over a mile, I repeated the technique I had used to carry the canoe across the first portage and it wasn't long until I began to feel like I was on a death march. My shoulders started combusting internally with the lactic acid build-up from the constant tension they were under, and my legs as well were straining under the relentless movement of the heavy load. When we finally got to Tuscarora, I collapsed.

"That was exhausting!" I exclaimed. "We have to take a break!"

"C'mon, rugby players don't take breaks," Jerome teased. "They keep playing until the whistle blows."

"Please?" I begged, and Jerome relented. We rested for fifteen minutes before putting our canoes back into the water and crossing over Tuscarora Lake. The next portage would take us to Owl Lake, and that's where Jerome showed me a better way to carry the canoe.

"First put your life jacket on," he instructed, and so I did. "Now, get under the canoe and rest the sidewalls on top of it."

"Like this?" I asked, maneuvering under the canoe and lowering the edges of the sidewalls onto the spots where the trap muscles meet the shoulders.

"Okay. Now put your arms forward like this."

Mimicking Jerome, I reached out my arms as if I were launching from a springboard into a dive and gripped the rims of the canoe. With the weight now resting over my torso instead of directly on my arms and shoulders, the canoe became much easier to transport. Soon I figured out that by lifting my arms I could easily raise the bow when I needed to see what lay ahead. For the first time, I noticed that someone had erected narrow goal-post structures along the portage path where you could place the tip of the canoe and easily back out from under it to allow for a moment's rest. I sure could have used that during the 366-rod portage to Tuscarora Lake!

The next three portages were really short as we made our way across Crooked, Tarry, and Mora Lakes to Little Saganaga Lake, a name we struggled to pronounce for the first couple of days until Jerome deemed "Little Sag" was sufficient. Despite its name, the lake was fairly large and deep, dotted with over a dozen islands, some of which contained camping pits. Jerome maneuvered us toward a spit of land that jutted out from about the midpoint of the convoluted southern shoreline, and there we found the fire pit that marked the campsite we would take up for the next six days.

Once we'd pitched the tents we eagerly set off to fish. While we all enjoyed catching fish, we'd upped the ante significantly by not packing-in any protein with our food supplies. That way we'd have to catch fish if we wanted to eat something other than instant pancake mix, instant oatmeal, bread, and crackers. Our first time out that afternoon put to rest any fears we might have harbored about enduring our expedition in a famished state. After paddling to a spot not too far from out campsite, the hits on our lures came quickly and soon the four of us had reeled in enough northern pike to make for a bountiful dinner by the campfire.

And so it went for the next three days: arise, boil water over a gas stove, make instant coffee, make oatmeal or cook up a batch of pancakes, clean camp, then head out to fish around and about the various waterholes of Little Sag, where we dreamed the great and more succulent tasting walleyes lay. After a short break for an afternoon siesta, we'd set out once more, always returning with a healthy catch to fry up in the cast iron skillet. We'd eat, clean camp again, and then bag up the food and hoist it into the tree branches, high enough to keep hungry bears from stealing it and far enough from the campsite to prevent an encounter with them in case they tried. As dusk settled in, we'd slather industrial-strength insect repellant on our skin to ward off the Mongol-sized hordes of mosquitoes, and don hats with veils of wispy netting hanging from the rims to add an extra barrier of protection. We'd finish off the day with a hypercompetitive game of cribbage before crawling into our sleeping bags and winding down with thoughtful chats before drifting off to sleep.

It seemed so idyllic, so carefree, but there were minor irritations—personality clashes, you might say—that everyone managed to keep under control, or at least under a façade of friendly forbearance, until Thursday came. Thursday was the day we decided to venture beyond Little Sag in order to check out the fishing in some of the neighboring lakes. We set out with a slightly overcast sky, barely noticing how quickly the smattering of clouds coalesced to blot out any remaining spots of the blue ceiling above.

We canoed about a mile and a half across Little Sag until we arrived at the southwest-most corner of the lake where we made a 140-rod portage to Elton Lake. I really lobbied hard to convince the group to go to that lake for no other reason except it was the same as the first name of Elton John, whose music I'd liked for many years. In hindsight, I suspect my insistence to go to *that* lake must have been somewhat annoying to my companions.

We fished a while there but no one got a bite; meanwhile, the sky continued to grow heavier and greyer. Bill and Jeff started grumbling, so I pulled out the map and showed Jerome there was another lake just south of Elton Lake we could check out, so we made our way to the next portage. It was short, but steep, and no sooner had we launched our canoes into the dark waters did the deluge begin. No smattering of drops or lightning flash or rumbling of thunder to announce the onset of precipitation, just an instantaneous downpour. We looked upward in surprise, as if we'd suddenly been transported to the foot of Niagara Falls to be pummeled by a relentless rush of water.

Like stoics, we tried not to react. We stayed on the water and fished, watching the turbulent lake surface bubble furiously, as if we were under siege by a thousand ravenous piranhas. We sat in silence for a long time, casting out our lines and reeling them in like animatronic figures in a wilderness exhibit.

I don't remember exactly how it started, but it was probably one of us saying something like, "This is stupid." I know myself well enough to admit it could have very easily been me to blurt out something like that. But then I do remember an argument broke out as to whether we should keep on fishing or head back to camp. Essentially, the disagreement was over whether we continued to endure the miserable pelting in the hope of catching some fish or we cut our losses on the investment of time and effort we made to get there in the first place and head back with empty stringers.

We didn't handle our dissent very well. Anybody that tried to offer something constructive got criticized. Then, after exchanging snipes, we'd clam up for a bit and sit in a sulk as we listlessly cast our lines and reeled them in. After a few moments, someone would let forth with an outburst of cursing, followed by snide remarks that cast aspersions toward each other's manhood. That precipitated more arguments, follower long periods of silence. Rinse and repeat.

Finally, Jerome said definitively, "We're going back. There're no fish here," and that made the defeat seem more acceptable.

Those were the last words anybody said as we withdrew from the lakes and backtracked the portages we'd made from Little Sag. The rain started to let up once we got back on the waters of Little Sag, and we stayed out long enough to catch four small northern pikes to eat for dinner, but it wasn't much, at least not like the previous days' catches.

The rain completely stopped when we paddled back to the shore of our campsite. The first thing I did was shed my rain gear and boots and climb into my sleeping bag, zipping it up as far as it would go and retracting my head inside like a turtle. I could hear some activity outside but I made no attempt to rise and go out to see what was going on or if help were needed. I fumed until I started dozing, then Jerome entered the tent without saying a word and crawled into his sleeping bag, too. After a while, he emerged from his down cocoon and climbed out of the tent, where he attempted unsuccessfully to build a fire to start cooking the meager catch of the day.

I didn't even want to get up to go eat, mainly because I didn't want the forced socialization of breaking bread together, such was my miserable condition. I ended up doing it anyway, and overcame my selfish withdrawal long enough to cook the fish we'd caught into a simple stew, motivated more by getting some food in my belly than anything else. I ate without saying much that evening, despite Jerome's compliments on how good the stew tasted, and I helped clean up afterwards, but that was about it. There was no cribbage game that evening, and no fireside chat. Everyone retired to their tents early.

The next morning brought sunshine—lots of it. For the first time since we'd put in, the sky was cloudless and the streaming rays of light started drying out the landscape. Instantly I felt better, making me wonder if maybe the lousy weather had been the source of all the misery the day before, a misery we couldn't bear alone so we attempted to shed it onto someone else. Now the glorious and warming rays of the sun dispelled all spirits of negativity and hostility. The new morning promised hope for the day, and standing there to sponge up the light and all its inviting glory, I felt shame for the way I had acted the day before. I kept respectfully quiet during breakfast but tried my best to be polite and congenial to my campmates, but could not yet bring myself to apologize.

The time came to push off in our canoes, and we worked our way over toward the western shores of Little Sag. After a couple of hours of fishing, we paddled over to a large outcropping of rocks that terraced the side of a steep bank and featured several large and horizontally flat boulders. This natural formation made the shore easily accessible from the water and offered a place to take a break.

I climbed onto the top of a large, rectangular-shaped piece of rock that rose about a foot above the water line and receded into an indeterminable depth beneath it. The flat surface invited me to recline and stretch, so I rolled over onto my side and extended myself fully, using the upper half of my arm to provide a cushion for my head. It started to get so warm that I had to remove my pullover. The heat radiating from the stone had a tranquilizing effect on me, and I started to get drowsy.

My mind drifted to prayer. In the semiconscious awareness of a holy God imbuing His presence in the bright morning light and how that seemed to expose my sinful attitude and behavior from the day before, I began to feel ashamed. I soon became aware of just how much work I had been doing to keep my shame suppressed so I wouldn't have to deal with it. I abandoned that effort once I realized the folly of pretending my bad behavior wasn't a big deal. I prayed to God for forgiveness for the way I'd acted, and in that fervent plea I realized my action was but a singular, sinful blemish on an entire landscape of depravity that was at the heart of who I was.

I needed cleansing, a washing away of this terrible sin-blot, work that only Jesus could do—and did do—when He died on account of it. I wanted to claim the forgiveness He made available through what He did for me on the cross, and I realized I had to undergo the baptism of repentance, just as John the Baptist had preached out in the wilderness (see Mark 1:4). However, this was not the Jordan River but the deep waters of Little Sag, and never mind that I had been baptized as an infant thirty-six years before. For the first time in my life I had an overpowering need of a tactile experience that I could associate with the faith I held in that long-ago event.

I opened one eye and looked out over the vast reservoir of water. I sat up and proceeded to unlace my boots, whipping them over the ankles of my feet and taking the socks with them. Still sitting on the rock, I unbuckled my belt and pushed and squirmed as the waistline of my pants traveled down the length of my legs, until they were completely removed.

"What are you doing?" Jerome asked.

"Repenting," I said. I stood and pulled my t-shirt over my head and jumped off the rock into the water.

A thermal black hole formed in the center of my body, sucking all the heat from my extremities into some remote spot in my core. I could have been in the middle of an ice cube, except that ice cubes float and I was sinking. I flailed my arms underwater and one of them touched the rock and I got enough of a grip with my hand to pull myself up and above the water's surface. A millisecond longer and I would have lost control over the gasp reflex and sucked in a lung full of icy liquid.

I scrambled quickly back onto the rock and stretched out, freezing cold and panting as if I had just run a hundred-meter sprint across the North Pole. But the rock felt warm, and so did the steady press from the sun above. I was lying flat, stomach side down, shoulders slightly twisted so my arms could stay positioned by my side, my left cheek pressed against the smooth granite, eyes closed. And I breathed and breathed and breathed, first rapidly, then slowly easing up, as I felt the shock of the plunge recede from my body and the temperature of my frame rise back to normal. A weird feeling came over me, like I was drifting away into slumber, yet maintaining complete awareness of my surroundings.

Then it happened. I stopped hearing my breathing and felt as if I were dissolving into the rock, only I was somewhere else, some place that I can only describe as the ground floor of perfect peace. It's like I stepped out of the fabric of reality as I knew it and into an enhanced realm of supernormal sensations, experiencing things I could never imagine, much less describe. I knew it intellectually, but for the first time in my life I became tacitly aware that God was the force behind all that existed, that His creative and sustaining power was in me, the rocks, the water, the sky, the whole universe—the unifying force making it real moment by moment and holding it all together. I felt lost and found at the same time—lost in an overwhelming sea of strange and marvelous vastitude but found in the close comfort of God's miraculous grace and life-imparting goodness. It was like my senses had been opened to a greater dimension beyond the familiar coordinates of time and space, a multi-dimensional universe of God's life-giving presence throughout the entirety of creation and all of the ages in which it has existed. I felt a joyful oneness with it all, a part of something much bigger and much better than I could ever be on my own.

"Are you all right?" Jerome asked, a slight chuckle in his voice.

In an instant I was back laying on the rock in nothing but a pair of soggy underwear. I was back so suddenly from whatever it was that I had experienced that it seemed at first like nothing had happened at all. Yet the impact of the experience was strong in my memory and I could not shake it. I knew better than try to explain it to Jerome and the others, and maybe it was for the better that I didn't, at least not at that moment. There is something to be said about keeping your most holy and intimate emotions to yourself, as if setting up a barrier between them and the rest of the world, kind of like the way the tabernacle curtain separated the Israelites from the Holy of Holies.

"Yeah," I answered as I got up and started getting dressed again, using the hooded fleece pullover to dry off any remaining wet spots that had not evaporated from the heat emanating out of the rock. "Hey, guys, I'm really sorry for the way I acted yesterday."

"We were all acting pretty bad," Jerome confessed.

"Yeah, but I was really bad," I replied. Thank goodness Jerome let it go there, or else it might have escalated into another argument of who was the worst.

We stayed up late that evening, talking around the campfire, listening to the doleful calls of loons echo from lake to lake. When the dark had finally settled in and bedtime approached, I stepped away from the campfire and headed into the woods a short distance to construct a makeshift latrine. As I walked through an opening in the canopy I saw my shadow appear on the ground, then move in a different direction, then disappear. I stopped dead in my tracks.

Now what? I thought. *First the experience on the rock, and now this—a shadow at nighttime that moves independent of me.* It happened again, and this time I looked skyward for the source that would create this strange effect and saw a brilliant panoply of green light suffuse across the heavens, collect in one spot, flare up, then dissipate, like a pitcher of glow-in-the-dark limeade spilling across the constellations of the nighttime firmament. It was the Northern Lights, so intensely bright that it formed shadows of me and the other objects around me. I took it as the punctuation mark to the day, an exclamation point so that I might never forget the lesson I learned.

It's funny, but God never seems to reveal himself to us when we are feeling spiritually aloft. More often it seems like He does it when we are miserable, suffering, confused or feeling helpless… when we least expect it. What happened that day in the Boundary Waters was a benevolent revelation, a first-hand understanding of what the Apostle Paul says in Colossians 1:17 when he speaks of the supremacy of Christ, "He is before all things, and in him all things hold together." (NIV) God cared enough for me to show me that beyond the forgiveness of my sins there is the promise of being in His holy presence, all because Jesus took those sins upon himself when He died on the cross, and made me righteous so that I could one day fully and eternally experience that glorious holy presence. Through God's grace I got a foretaste of the peace and joy that eternal association will bring. The powerful memory of that experience in the Boundary Waters would provide reassurance to me of God's presence and grace during the many trials in my life that were yet to come.

SWEPT AWAY

August 9, 2014

After all of us had received the anointing oil, Cliff then imparted to us some practical advice. "It's not unusual for emotions to come out during a time like this. If it happens to you when you're speaking, just go with it for the moment and don't try to shut it down. It will pass and everyone will understand, and everything will be all right."

That possibility had not occurred to me, but the advice seemed sound. Nevertheless, I silently prayed to God that this would not happen to me while I was up there, since the last thing I wanted was for attention to be drawn to me and diverted from Brian's memory. Then Cliff and Aaron led us in an open prayer, and we left for the worship center.

As I reached the top of the stairs, I ran into Keesha Johnson, whom I hadn't talked to since the night of the accident. "Hold up for a second," she said, and she proceeded to tie a string bracelet around my left wrist. It was a gesture of remembrance for Brian, who wore about a half-dozen such string bracelets around his wrist at all times, one for each mission trip he'd served on during his lifetime. I decided it was going to be a reminder for me to keep Dena and the girls in my thoughts and prayers.

I finally made it to the pew where our seats were saved. Debbie and Zack were there, and around us were about 700 people, most of them packed into the main area of the worship center, and the rest seated in the overflow area. This was a large crowd for Lewiston, certainly one of the largest I'd ever been assembled with inside a church. I pulled out the purple-inked manuscript and looked over it, and saw a few more areas that needed amending. I was astonished at how the Holy Spirit was still guiding me around what to say, even this close to saying it. Debbie gave me a pen and I made the revisions.

The service started and Aaron made some welcoming remarks and outlined what would be taking place over the next two hours. He finished by cryptically stating that we would even hear from Brian himself at the conclusion of the service. I had no idea what that meant, and before I could presuppose anything Cliff took the stage and had us all rise to sing.

It was not hard to lift up my voice in worship during the first song. My heart was both broken at the loss of my friend and yet full of gratitude for a God that provided eternal hope in times like this; thus, the music was the conduit for healing the hurt and giving thanks to a great and magnificent redeemer. When the song finished, Dan and Todd took the stage for scripture reading and prayer. Then there was a slideshow highlighting Brian's life and family, after which Gary Grabow came up and read Brian's obituary.

Cliff and the band members started the second song, one I knew well from worship services at the Lutheran church I belonged to in Spokane, David Crowder's "How He Loves." Our pastor's son often performed this when he led song team, and the passion he put into that song testified to his unwavering belief in the message it delivered. It wasn't a performance; it was a musical expression of faith. Now, as the familiar words rang through the Nazarene Church, the extent of God's love as embodied in the lyrics became very real to me. My voice started breaking up and tears started flowing from my eyes. For a moment I thought I needed to fight it, to maintain control in front of all of these people, but then I remembered the advice Cliff gave us in his office. I gave up and suddenly found myself no longer able to sing. I was so overcome that I had to hold onto Debbie as my eyes poured forth the well of tears that had filled up so deeply inside over the course of the past seven days. I began heaving and sobbing, as grief poured out of me in giant waves.

Then, an astonishing thing happened. I began to sense an inexplicable joy pouring into me at the same time. I was weeping for the death of my friend, but the song was reminding me that God's love made it such that death was not the end of the story. That love had conquered death when God sacrificed his son, Jesus Christ, for our sins on the cross at Calvary, only to raise him up from the dead three days later, so that we would believe in Him and also have eternal life. For that reason I had much to celebrate in the midst of this devastating grief, but could hardly express any of this amid the riptide of emotions that had rendered me helpless and swept me away.

The song ended and I started to recover my faculties as the next couple of speakers made the trek up to the lectern to give their testimonies about Brian. One of the most touching things the assembly witnessed was Brian's youngest daughter, Alicia, and her heartfelt goodbye to her daddy, which she read from a hand-written manuscript. Then my turn came. I prayed before leaving the pew, then climbed onto the stage and stood in front of the lectern, and began giving the message God had led me to prepare. I was aware of His power, strength, and direction within me as I spoke, hardly needing to look at the purple words any more.

EULOGY

My name is Ike Andrews, I am honored and humbled that God brought Brian into my life as a friend.

I'd like to read to you from 1 Samuel 20, verses 41-42:

After the boy had gone, David got up from the south side of the stone and bowed down before Jonathan three times, with his face to the ground. Then they kissed each other and wept together—but David wept the most. Jonathan said to David, "Go in peace, for we have sworn friendship with each other in the name of the Lord, saying, 'The Lord is witness between you and me, and between your descendants and my descendants forever.'" Then David left, and Jonathan went back to town.

Last Wednesday, as I reflected on the events of this past week, this passage from 1 Samuel came to mind. Like David, I said goodbye to Brian last Sunday morning and wept. David and Jonathan were two men who epitomized friendship like no other two men in history. Long before the events of this week ever happened, I had come to realize that Brian was like a Jonathan to me.

If he was that kind of friend to me, I can imagine what he was to these men assembled here.

I can scarcely imagine what kind of friend he was to those people so important in his life, those he loved and associated with every day: his wife, Dena, and precious daughters Ashley, Amber and Alicia, and other members of his family.

Have you ever wondered how Brian got that capacity to love and serve and spread goodwill to so many people?

Brian was totally open to the Holy Spirit, that's how. The Holy Spirit infused him, guided his life, and became a beacon of God's love in the darkness that is in this world. Matthew 5: 13 – 16 says, "You are the light of the world. A city on a hill cannot be hidden. Neither do people light a lamp and put it under a bowl. Instead they put it on its stand, and it gives light to everyone in the house. In the same way let your light shine before men, that they may see your good deeds and praise your Father in heaven."

Let me tell you some of the ways that that light shined through Brian.

Brian's light shined every time he talked about the things he did with his family. One of the last text messages I got from him was about how he finally got Dena to go downhill mountain biking with him at McCall. There was so much exuberance in that small box of words, and I could just see him beaming with pride when he told me Dena did awesome. Brian and his family were frequent guests in our home. My wife Debbie and I remember the many times he would sit on our couch in the living room after a day of doing something with his girls up in Spokane. There was so much delight and passion in his voice as he told about their volleyball matches, or shopping for prom dresses or point shoes. It was no different from the way he talked us about his extreme sports adventures, like backcountry skiing down fresh powder on a remote mountain in the Wallowa's with his friend Jeremy. His face lit up every time he talked about his daughters. He was so focused on their lives and being in the moment when he was with them.

Brian's light shined in the mission fields of Seattle, Ecuador, Madagascar and Guatemala. He sacrificed his vacation time from work to be the hands and feet of Jesus in the world. Strong hands and feet, as I might add, given the amount of work he and others put into the structures they were building for their brothers and sisters in Christ. I remember seeing a picture of Brian all pumped up after a day of work on one of those mission sites. His light was also a magnet to the children of those remote areas. I remember the time he told me about when he was just kicking the soccer ball by himself in a vacant lot in Madagascar when before he knew it a multitude of boys showed up wanting to join him and they ended up in an impromptu soccer match.

Brian's light shined before every trail ride when he assembled us all together around our mountain bikes and offered up prayers for the ride. He gave thanks and glory to God for allowing us to have the physical capacity to enjoy such unique recreation in his creation, and he also prayed for protection, for the proper functioning of our bikes, for fellowship and—most importantly for him—for delivering us safely back home to our families at the end of the ride.

Brian's light shined whenever he helped a friend or stranger in need. How many of you have been helped by Brian at one or more times in your life? The countless service projects that he's done for others through this church's Movers & Shakers group have inspired me to join with Debbie and other brothers and sisters in Christ at Redeemer Lutheran Church in Spokane to start a similar ministry called Helping Hands & Hearts.

Brian's light shined whenever he overcame fear. Several years ago Brian and I went on a weekend mountain-biking adventure in the McCall area with our mutual friend, Carl Strong. Saturday was a ride on a snowy course on 20-mile trail near Upper Payette Lake, while Sunday was an adrenalin adventure at the newly opened downhill course at the Tamarack Resort. At one point during the day, Brian led us off the blue square trails to a double-black diamond trail. We rode a few yards down the entrance to the trail then stopped suddenly at the edge of a small cliff. What little bit of a trail there was exposed on the cliff face was interrupted by large rocks and a narrow crevice. Carl and I backed our bikes away from the edge and took the escape route, but Brian stayed at the top. As best as I can remember, we watched from the bottom of the cliff as Brian focused on the trail, squeezing his eyes and gritting his teeth. A couple of times he rolled backwards as if to give up, but after wavering, we saw a look of fearlessness sweep over his face. He sat back as far as the seat would allow and rolled his front wheel over the edge. He plunged down the dirt part and as the first large rock loomed he lifted the front wheel so he could land on it, and then timed the brakes perfectly to come to a complete standstill. From there, he bunny-hopped over the crevice to another rock, where he kept his balance until he could make enough small, clockwise hops to position his front wheel so it faced downhill again. Then he jumped back onto the trail past the crevice, and rolled over the rest of the rocks until he had made his way to the foot of the cliff. It was the most astonishing feat of skill

I have ever witnessed and demonstrated to me what an amazing athlete God had gifted Brian to be.

You know, at the beginning of this message I told you Brian was like a Jonathan to me. As the Holy Spirit helped me reflect on this message, I began to think that maybe it was the other way around. Maybe I should be saying Brian was like a David to me. In Acts 13:22, the apostle Paul recounts this: "After removing Saul, [God] made David their king. He testified concerning him: 'I have found David son of Jesse a man after my own heart; he will do everything I want him to do.'"

What does it mean to be a man after God's own heart, especially in this age where the idea of manhood is under attack by the world? You know what I mean. Movies, TV and advertising portraying men as helpless fools or idiots.

Let me tell you about some things that lead me to believe Brian was like a David and a man after God's own heart.

A man after God's own heart is pure in heart. I think most of you know how much Brian was into sports and physical activity, especially CrossFit. At one time he had a subscription to Muscle and Fitness magazine. He read it for ideas for new exercise routines and motivation. Then the magazine's production staff decided they could sell more issues by having a scantily clad female on the cover posing with a body builder, often suggestively. Brian stopped the subscription. He didn't want any image in his house that would dishonor his pledge of fidelity that he made to Dena at the altar, nor did he want to send the wrong message to his daughters that women are to be valued only for their sexual attractiveness. Brian was pure in heart.

A man after God's own heart is a man who is forgiving. I once made a foolish vow to God that if he would help me through a painful period of my life, I would give up something that I dearly loved to do. As I lay there suffering, the only thing I could think of that I dearly loved to do was going mountain biking with Brian. Eventually I got through the pain, but struggled to keep the vow. I was inexplicably silent when Brian would ask me to go riding with him. After about two months, I could take it no more, and I agreed to join him with Carl on Moscow Mountain. We met Brian at the bottom of Moscow Mountain Road, and shuttled to the top of the mountain. On that twenty-minute ride up, I told him what I had done, and I asked for his forgiveness for being so deceptive about my motives during that time. He forgave me without flinching. Instantly our mountain-biking companionship was restored just like it was before, like the incident never happened. Of course, I had to go to God and ask for his forgiveness, too. Then, about a year ago, I realized Brian had been a James 5:16 in my life, not just then but other times as well: James 5:16 says, "Therefore, confess your sins to each other and pray for each other so that you may be healed. The prayer of a righteous man is powerful and effective." Brian was forgiving.

A man after God's own heart is a man who shows kindness to all of God's children. I can't think of a better way to illustrate this than the following story posted on Facebook by Kelly Cach, who graciously gave me permission to share with you this story about Brian and her daughter Nora:

Brian and Nora had a special relationship. He called her his "Little Buddy." At chapel every month, [he would say] "There's my little buddy." At Costco, at school events, at gatherings, or just stopping by their home, "There's my little buddy." He'd let her touch his soul patch...she loves mustaches and beards. He'd sit behind her at Chapel and they'd make up silly games, like "I'll throw all of the things on the floor, and you pick them up." She'd steal his phone, and he'd let her. And they always ended with a "High-five, knuckles, blow it up!" Recently, at Art Under the Elms, we ran into Brian and some of his family members. "There's my little buddy," he'd said. Without skipping a beat, Nora responded, "Hi, Brian!" (High-five, knuckles, blow it up!). May not seem like much, but for a child with Down syndrome, speaking clearly and calling someone by name is a big deal. He made an impression on her. After receiving the tragic news Sunday morning, another dear mutual friend shared something with me. She said, "Did you know that after Nora was born and the Johnson's heard the news of [Nora's] Down's syndrome, Brian said, "That is so cool!" And I'm sure he said it with his big contagious smile on his face and excitement in his voice. Because Brian knew "cool." He knew it before we did. That statement was so telling of their future special friendship.

Brian was kind to all of God's children. In honor of Brian's playful spirit, I'd like for you to turn to the person next to you and "high-five" them and say, "For Brian!"

A man after God's own heart is a man who is devoted to God's word. Brian's appetite for God's message grew year after year. I've saved most of the emails that Brian and I exchanged since 2006. There are well over 1000 of them, filling 373 pages in a Word document. Granted, most of the discussion threads relate to arranging our next mountain-biking adventure, or describing the previous one. But almost 900 of those words in those emails are words like God, Spirit, Pray, Jesus, Lord, Worship, Faith. As the years went by, Brian started forwarding more devotional materials that inspired him and taught him about God's kingdom. Even on our overnight mountain-biking adventures, Brian took along the Word. Once we went to Ketchum to ride the Imperial Gulch trail. One hour into the trail his derailleur broke. As we scrambled to repair it enough to allow us to get out, a ferocious storm broke loose and raged marble sized hailstones down upon us. We escaped over ball bearings of ice until the hail melted and turned the singletrack into a sluice of mud. Rain utterly soaked every fiber of our being. In our desperation to get back to where we had parked more quickly, we took an unknown trail that looked to be a short cut, only to find ourselves speeding around a curve and suddenly facing a twenty-foot deep ravine with no time to stop and the only means across being a railroad tie…and that was just the morning ride! After all that happened that day, most men would go straight to a stiff shot of whisky, but Brian was content to sit down by the feeble camp fire we had built with wet wood and read his Bible by the fading late June light. Brian was devoted to God's word.

Lastly, and probably most important to Brian, a man after God's own heart is a warrior. Not the kind of man who loves to fight and seeks confrontation, but someone who is conscious that the ultimate battle to be fought in this world is against the forces of evil, led by Satan. In Brian's testimony, he compares his past spiritual life to sitting on the bench in a baseball game. Life was easy, and very little happened. Then he talks about how things changed when he stepped up to the plate to get into the game, realizing that whenever he makes a decision for God, the enemy likes to strike. I'll give you a specific example of this: Once, as he was preparing to leave for one of his overseas mission trips, his car broke down, the oven stopped working and the basement flooded all at the same time. Talk about putting some heavy stress on someone! But Brian was onto the Devil's schemes, and not only was he a brave fighter in the realm of spiritual warfare, he was also a prayer warrior, unhesitant to drop to his knees and petition the Lord for any matter, big or small. Nor was he afraid to ask for reinforcements in the battle. Many times Brian leaned on his brothers for all kinds of prayers requests, many of which I saw God honor. Brian was a warrior.

Some might think the forces of darkness orchestrated this tragedy to Brian's life and being. We don't know for sure. We do know from the book of Job that such things can happen. But what defeats Satan in his schemes is God's ability to bring so much good from what seems like so much heartache. Think about how this has brought all of us together to honor a man whose life brings glory to God, to reflect on those characteristics that make a difference in this world, and to convict us to surrender our lives in service to God, just like he did. Think about how Brian brought a new life and a new hope to the unknown recipients of the organs that he donated. It's not too much different than how God took the tragic death of Jesus Christ and turned that into a new life and hope for all of us. Because Jesus died for our sins on the cross, we have received the gift of eternal life. Do we now understand the grief that the disciples, the two Marys, and the other followers felt when our Lord was crucified? And because we know what happens next in the story, should we not now celebrate in our hope in Jesus Christ, who will bring us into his glory one day, and reunite us with Brian?

Until then, we say farewell to a man of many facets: Loving husband, devoted father, beloved friend, blessed son, spiritual leader, valued employee, competitive teammate, fearless outdoor adventurer, faithful servant, eternal child of God. Brian Matthew Johnson, rest in God's peace and in His loving arms. We will see you again someday in God's glorious kingdom. Amen.

I AM SECOND

When I had finished speaking, it was Jeremy's turn. He told an anecdote about a time he and Brian made a long trip to Oregon for some backcountry skiing which would have made another chapter in the book I was writing had I been along. I would have titled it "Sacrifice," since Brian stopped to help some people stuck in the snow along the way to the trailhead and it ended up taking all the time he and Jeremy had available to ski just to help them out. Jeremy admitted he was frustrated with the way things turned out, but such was the character of Brian that he was glad that they had simply been there to help them.

Lastly, Aaron took the stage to speak a few words to conclude the service. He first announced that the number of people who had benefitted from Brian's donated organs stood at eighty-one. The air pressure in the room must have dropped several millibars as the congregation collectively gasped in astonishment. I had pegged the total number at eight, thinking that lungs, heart, kidneys, corneas and liver were all that mattered, but apparently tendons, stem cells and other parts were helping a multitude of others as well. The tragic death of one man brought a chance to new life to many, just as Jesus's tragic death on the cross brought the hope for new life to all.

Then Aaron revealed the way we were going to hear from Brian that day. He told the story about how I had entrusted Brian's laptop to Jared and how Jared had been able to recover Brian's "I Am Second" testimony, never before given until now. As Aaron began reading, Brian's words spoke to the assembled and gave the final seal of assurance that he was in the loving arms of His Heavenly Father.

I was born into a Christian family. My parents took me to church at a young age. My earliest memories of church were of me as Joseph in the Christmas play. I memorized verses like every other Sunday school kid and accepted Christ into my heart because my teachers said I should. I remember one challenge in Sunday school was if we memorized enough verses, our teacher would take us to see the Seattle SuperSonics. Well that was motivation enough for me. I memorized the required number and myself and several students went to the Kingdome to see the Sonics play. Pretty cool for a little kid.

Growing up, sports was a big part of my life. I started out with baseball and then found soccer. Soccer was my sport. I was good at it and continue to play to this day. Volleyball was another sport I took up and fell in love with. Again, I play volleyball to this day. When I was nine or ten my dad took me down to his buddy's motorcycle shop and we bought my first motorcycle. I couldn't believe it. My own motorcycle. It was a Honda XL75. We took it home and I did figure eights in the front yard until I wore a path. We lived on several acres of pasture and forest. The neighbor kids had motorcycles too so we all rode in a little gang together. It was a great time growing up as a kid.

Towards the end of my sixth grade, my dad received a call from a guy who said he was his long lost brother. We were all shocked to say the least. The man talked of being raised by his dad, but had no knowledge of his mom. He hired a company that finds people and through a series of events, they found my dad. My dad started doing some research on his own to find out what this was all about. His mom had passed away several years before, so he started asking other relatives. Sure enough, he was able to piece together what had happened. His mom had been married three different times and had three different boys. This was the middle brother of the three. Of course my dad wanted to get to know his "new" brother. They visited us and we visited them. Soon my parents decided they wanted to move out of the Seattle area and be closer to our new family. So that summer after sixth grade we packed up and moved to sunny Lewiston, Idaho.

As exciting as it was to move to a new state, starting at a new school wasn't, especially junior high. I wasn't the type to make new friends quickly so it was difficult. My parents started church shopping and finally landed one they enjoyed. The problem for me was, there were no other teenagers my age. I quickly became uninterested in church. Nothing seemed to apply to me. Once I started high school and got a job, I stopped going to church.

My first taste of alcohol was my senior year of high school. My best friend had a brother in college so it was easy to get anything we wanted to drink. His parents were divorced, with his dad living in another state and his mom working long hours, so we spent a lot of time at his house. Weekends we'd find where the party was and hit it. We didn't do drugs but drank plenty enough. I really didn't like the taste, but since this is what my friend was doing, that's what I did. I was wearing a mask. School was easy for me, so I received good grades, but I wasn't making great choices outside of school on my own.

After high school, five of us all went to college together and rushed through the same fraternity, Farmhouse at the University of Idaho. Drinking and partying continued to intensify. This time however my grades were starting to suffer. By the end of my freshman year I had to make a decision. I decided to leave the fraternity and school and transfer to Lewis Clark State College. In one weekend I found an apartment and a job. I began my life on my own. After high school my parents moved back to the Seattle area. So, my parents moved away from me, kinda funny when I think about it.

I finished college, receiving my B.S. in Business Administration. After college I married my high school sweetheart and we started living life as a married couple. Soon after we decided to start a family and Ashley came along. For most of this time life was easy. No big deal. I still believed in God, but lived my life as my own. I remember thinking, there'll be time for God later, when I'm older. Like I said, life seemed easy, no big deal. That was soon to change. The job I was working at came upon tough times. They needed to let someone go, but being a small family owned business, it was difficult to decide who that would be. It didn't take me long to figure out it should be me. I was young, mobile, with a college degree, so I told my boss I would resign. He became emotional and said this was the toughest decision he had to make and would have to accept my resignation. I drove home realizing the enormity of what just happened. I had no job, no prospects for a job, no money and wife and 6-month-old baby. What was I going to do now? I arrived at my apartment, told my wife and we broke down together. I remember praying to God about my situation and immediately felt the weight of what happened lifted from my shoulders. It was one of the first times I remember God taking total control of me. I started job hunting, interviewing jobs I thought I was a shoe-in for, but kept getting turned down. I started doubting my abilities and wondering why I couldn't get a job. Then one day my friend called me saying she found a job for me in the back of a magazine. Oh this should be good, I thought. She told about the job and said she knew the manager. So I sent in a cover letter and my resume, not thinking much about it. A week or so later, I received a call asking if I could do a lunch interview. I said yes. A piece of advice about a lunch interview: don't go hungry. There were two of them interviewing me. One would ask a question while the other ate. Once I finished answering his question, the other would ask me one. I don't remember eating much of my meal. The interview must have gone well because a couple days later I was asked to come out for a more formal interview. I did, meeting with several people and answered a bunch of questions. It seemed like it went well, but I wasn't sure. A few days later I received a call asking if I'd be interested in coming to work for them. I about dropped the phone. In college you dream about landing a job that does the certain things you enjoy and getting paid for it. This was that job for me. Seventeen years and six months later, I still enjoy what I'm doing. I now realize why I didn't get any of the other jobs I thought I was a shoe-in for. God was preparing me for something greater than I could hope for. Another lesson learned.

So I had this great job that God landed for me, but it wasn't enough for me to put Him first. We wanted to raise our children in church, so we started attending First Church of the Nazarene, where Dena grew up in as a "bus kid." I went to Church, but was still good at wearing a mask. I said the right things, but I hung out in the background. Dena became involved so I would help her, not really putting much more effort in.

At thirty, I had a bilateral sagittal split osteotomy. In other words, a broken jaw. I wish I had a great story of how I broke it, but I don't. It was on purpose, as part of my orthodontic treatment. It was outpatient surgery in Spokane. The doctor said he wasn't going to tell me how he was going to do it, so I still don't know to this day. Something about this physical break to my body spurred something in me to make a spiritual break. It was time to stop putting God off and make him first. After my jaw healed up, I rededicated my life to Christ. My first act as a "new" Christian was to attend a men's retreat. It was great for me to listen to all these other guys share their faith and experiences. I started attending a weekly men's Bible study, I joined the Church's annual Easter Play, taking on a major roll, all because I started stepping out in faith in response to God's prompting. My friend gave me The Message Bible. I read it from *cover to cover. The first time I had ever read the Bible completely. It was amazing, like reading a novel. So much more came alive upon reading this version. It's exactly what I needed.*

Something else happened though. I was punched in the face, figuratively speaking. Everything seemed to be falling apart. Everything I touched went south. I couldn't figure out why. Then something we were reading in our men's group opened my eyes to what was going on. This is how I describe it. For most my spiritual life I was riding the bench of a baseball team. On the bench, life was easy. No big deal. But once I jumped off the bench, grabbed a bat and stepped up to the plate, that all changed. I was now in the game, ready to make a difference, and the enemy did not like that. The first pitch was high inside, aiming for my head, causing me to fall back into the dirt. I got back up and received a similar pitch. Now that I realized where the trouble was coming from, it gave me a new perspective on life. I was able to press into God and ask for His help. God answered. He led me through those troubled times. This started a pattern that still happens to this day. Whenever I make a decision for God, the enemy likes to strike. I continue to press into God, and He carries me through it.

My story isn't over. New chapters are being written continually. By putting God first and stepping out in faith, I've reaped the rewards over and over again. As I get older, I can sense God talking to me, and I've learned to listen and enjoy the outcome. Watching how God works, it becomes easier to lean on him, when all seems impossible. My favorite verse is Philippians 4:13: "I can do all things through Christ who gives me strength." This has carried me through some difficult times and situations.

My challenge to you is, no matter your story, God has a plan for you. He's just waiting for you to say yes, and begin the adventure with him.

My name is Brian Johnson and I AM SECOND!

And with that the service ended, for what else could be said after hearing Brian's own testimony? One by one the crowd that was there to honor Brian's memory started heading out of the worship center and to the backyard, where the tent was set up with the barbecue lunch. I stayed behind and I talked and listened to a lot of folks. Many of them had their own special memories of Brian that they wanted to share with me and I was humbled at the additional testimony to his character that these anecdotes provided.

However, one individual had a story that wasn't about Brian. Nevertheless it was an astonishing admission of how God had worked in her life that week on my behalf. Kelly Paynter, an acquaintance from the Congregational Presbyterian Church we attended when we lived in Clarkston, approached me.

"Ike," she began, "I had no idea you would be speaking today but the Holy Spirit has been prompting me all week to pray for you, and so I did."

"Whoa!" I uttered, nearly dumbstruck. I silently reflected on how many times God had sustained me during the past seven days. "Those prayers made a difference," I said knowingly. "Thank you so much."

We talked a little longer then said goodbye. As Kelly walked to her car, I paused to reflect on how great God was that He would move her to offer up prayers for me when I most needed them. I realized I had done very little in the way of asking others to pray for me during the past seven days, so God was providing even when I was slack in making my requests known.

At length I caught up with Carl, who had ridden down from Spokane on his motorcycle to attend the service. Zack joined us and we made our way over to partake of the barbecue that the volunteers from the church were still serving. The talking and listening continued, and I lingered around until the very end so I could spend a few moments with Dena and the girls before leaving. I hugged them and showed them the string bracelet that Keesha had tied around my wrist, which I pledged would be a reminder to me to pray for them.

Debbie asked Zack if he would ride back to Spokane with her, so I made the two-hour trip home in silent contemplation of all that had happened since the night of the accident. I marveled at how many times God had been faithful to my prayers for help in dealing with the many obstacles and challenges that had beset me. I tried to remember an equally condensed time span in my life where I had witnessed and experienced so many miraculous interventions by God in my life and others, but I couldn't. How awesome is our God that He would minister to us frail humans at such a time as this, when so many of us needed His assurance that death is not the end of the trail on this adventure called life, but a beginning of a wonderful, eternal, and worshipful existence with the Creator of our universe.

EPILOGUE

September 7th, 2014

About a month had passed, and even though things weren't "normal" anymore without Brian around, the other normalcies of life have a way of reasserting themselves over you. Just as the memories of the wondrous events of God's divine intervention were starting to fade, a friend directed me to a Facebook posting by a woman whom I had never heard of before. Her name was Melody Paasch, and she founded an online school called, "Now, Interpret This." The school's stated purpose is to provide "training in sensitivity to the heart of Creator God and delivering His thoughts by His Spirit." This is what Melody wrote:

Saturday evening, August 2, 2014 the interns and I were driving back to Colfax, WA from Palouse Falls during our Summer Intern Retreat. There were eleven of us in four different vehicles, heading back to our hotel. While at the falls, we prayed briefly over the river, the land and the region. We made a deposit there on the land as well. Interesting, that it was soil and elements of the land from our own homes, which we sensed secured spiritual authority for our prayer initiative. One of the interns had received this direction for us, having no idea at the time what it was for. After our prayer, I had a strong sudden nudge that we were done, and should leave right away. Each of us climbed into the cars and prayed protection over our return for the night.

Along the way, a couple of our seers saw angels accompanying our vehicles with their swords out-stretched. To our surprise, we quickly came upon a terrible accident. It had just taken place. A mini-van had swerved to miss some deer on the road; and that van carrying a precious family of five, spun out of control and flipped. When we arrived the husband was still in the car, the oldest daughter had been thrown many feet out into a dark rocky ditch. It took a while to find her. The wife and other two daughters were banged up, but fine.

We waited for over thirty minutes before the arrival of the ambulance, as each of our eleven took a post. There was little conversation and little need for instruction. We just all knew where to be and where we were called to minister. This was a stunning picture of unity! We each reported to our commissioned post to pray. Each believing in faith that God's hand was on this husband and all of his family.

The Lord sent, not only the eleven interns with me to pray, but also other travelers who loved and trusted God to pray and cover them. The family was surrounded by random believers sending prayers to the throne. Each one doing whatever was needed to help. The medics were all aware of our work and cordially released us to our duties as we carefully stayed out of their way. Even asking some of us for help at times. It was obvious that they could only do so much, as was conveyed in their kind regard toward each of us.

We were in the middle of nowhere, and even the medics were improvising until they could get this man to a care flight for his hospital transport. They couldn't get the helicopter where we were, and there were only very small hospitals in the area and they too, were not that close. We were all there for nearly an hour before the ambulances got Brian and his oldest daughter off to the hospital.

No one left their post the whole time. We had interns stationed at the rear, who remained in the car to pray. Some were waving flags on the side of the highway, doing spiritual warfare on the family's behalf. Still others were with Ashley in the ditch and others covered Amber, the daughter who had been driving. Some went back and forth between the daughters, the wife and Brian; declaring all trauma be broken off each of them and calling life into Brian's physical body.

One intern saw the four in the car with her, in the heavenly court room before The Father as advocates for the family. She sensed that the reason for the previous dirt release at the falls, was to secure the authority that we needed to pray on the land for this family. Then she got the glory flags out of the car, which another intern constructed, and several began to wave them in the air. The passers-by watched the glittering flags snapping in the wind in the beams of their headlights, with awe and curiosity. We were truly on assignment!

Back on the scene, one of the interns played old hymns on her harmonica over Brian as the medics worked to keep him with us. The other four unknown travelers each had their place as well, and not one left before the ambulances. The whole scene of this corporate response was eloquently orchestrated by the hand of God. No one could have planned what we all witnessed that night. Several of us saw Brian take leave of his body, but continued to speak life to the situation.

Brian was a mere forty-three years of age, and we knew in our hearts that his family needed him. We believed that God had covered this family, as He had covered all those He had ordained to be there at that very moment to offer comfort, encouragement, and prayer. We later heard that Brian was pronounced brain dead upon arrival to the hospital. His skull had been crushed and he had only been semi-conscious the whole time we were with him at the scene of the accident.

What we didn't know was that he was an organ donor. Upon arrival, the hospital placed him on life support to preserve his organs. To our deep sadness, Sunday morning he went home to be with Jesus. We knew that we had all done everything required of us, on his behalf. Later, at his memorial celebration, we learned that he was a passionate lover of God and an extreme sports adventurer, a loving husband and extraordinary father.

He had apparently kept his body in such excellent condition, that a reported eighty-one people received life or help at Brian's departure. There are actually eighty-one people who now carry a part of Brian Johnson's DNA! He lives on in the many bodies and lives of his donor recipients. That is surely abundant life!

Something later became quite clear to me, while sitting with friends visiting about a similar event. I could suddenly see that one of the things Papa had used us for that night, was to cleanse the memory of Brian's DNA. Little did we know, that Brian's tissue and organs were going to bring life to others, who might have experienced the torment of his trauma. Our tissues and cells have memory, you know. Just as our brains do.

It has been established in many cases, that those who receive organ donations at times, suffer the memory of the subsequent shock of the violence and death of their donor. We had all been there coming against the memory of any trauma, not only in the lives of Brian's family, but in his body as well. Not only is there possibility of the donor recipient experiencing the trauma that the donor suffered, but the redemption of this is that they can also receive the anointing and gifts that were within him.

Wow!!! We release the anointing of Brian Johnson to each of his donor recipients now! He was a kind, loving, and loyal friend, who directed others to Jesus.

We could have never known at the time what impact we and the others might have had in the spirit realm. Now, having more understanding of just one of God's initiatives, this seems even more amazing than I or any of us could have imagined. What a revelation! This is the way our God works, on every side of every situation and on every level and dimension of what is needed. He is so intentional in all that He does. Thank you, Lord for using us and the others you pulled off the road in the darkness of your "Secret Service" that night. We are among those honored to be in Brian's presence, for even just a moment.

When I finished reading this, I was stunned. For one thing, Melody's vision of Brian taking leave of his body confirmed what I had realized that fateful night in the waiting room next to the ICU when Dena repeated the details of her supernatural encounter with Brian on the drive to Spokane, which Dan LejaMeyer had told me about earlier. But on a grander scale, I began to see a much larger spiritual orchestration of events that started that evening and lasted throughout the whole week, culminating that morning during Brian's service. It reinforced in me that God truly does care about us as evidenced through all the many ways he touched other's lives and mine during that tumultuous week. He allowed us to glimpse the miraculous ways he works in our lives, giving us the privilege to validate our faith in him, just when we most needed the reassurance of hope in his promises.

I changed as a result of what happened to my best friend. First of all, a part of me died with Brian, the part that only Brian could bring out whenever I was in his presence. It was a bold and masculine spirituality, a wildness in heart both for God and adventure. It's still in me, but it's rare that it's expressed like it was when I was around Brian. Next, I grasped how short life is and how God has given me gifts and talents and a set amount of time to use them in His service. Only by dedicating my life to Him will I completely understand his sovereignty and the role I play in bringing about His will. Life has meaning and purpose, and following God's path is a far better trail to ride than the one the world goads you to travel.

Paraphrasing Matthew 7:13-14 with regard to the sport of mountain biking, there comes a point where you have to steer yourself off the broad highway and hit the trailhead for a ride on the narrow singletrack. There are a lot of bad habits you have to shed to become a really good rider on that trail, but God is there to fix things right if you just keep yielding to that internal GPS (God's Providential Spirit; that is, the Holy Spirit) that He bestows upon all his children.

While the singletrack leads to the same destination, it's a different ride for everybody, with both common and unique obstacles and challenges. Finding your line and keeping your eye on it at all times is fraught with many distractions that can steer you off course for a while and set you back. But there are lessons to be learned from these setbacks, and the hills and valleys you traverse along the way make for the ride of a lifetime. When you reach the end of the trail, you are welcomed home into the arms of your father and creator, who's first words to you will be, "Well done, good and faithful rider!"

I don't ride as much now as I did when Brian was alive, but I will never forget the friendship and the lessons from the trail that he and I and others learned from our experiences out there. This book is dedicated to him and his memory, and to a great and glorious God who makes all things good for those who love Him.

APPENDIX

A PHOTO ALBUM OF PEOPLE AND PLACES MENTIONED IN THIS BOOK

Brian Johnson and family at Swallows Nest Park, Clarkston, WA, Autumn 2013. From left: Brian, Alicia, Amber, Dena, Ashley (and Lily). (Photo courtesy of Dena Johnson.)

Turkey Bowl Participants, 2006. Every Thanksgiving a group of men from the First Church of the Nazarene in Lewiston, Idaho would get together for a competitive game of football. In 2006 Brian invited the author, who brought along his son and neighbor. Mentioned in this book are (kneeling) Dan LejaMeyer (2nd from left), the author (center), Brian Johnson (right end); (standing) Bob Dice (3rd from left), Todd Johnson (center), Zack Andrews and Jim Gentry (next two men after Todd). (Photo by Brian Johnson.)

The author on Contour Trail, Moscow Mountain, September 2007. (Photo by Brian Johnson.)

Brian and Jeremy Carr at the summit of Mt. Hood, OR, May 2006. (Photo courtesy of Jeremy Carr.)

Enjoying the NAIA World Series in Lewiston, ID, Memorial Day Weekend, 2014. From left: Steph Middleton, Dena, Brian and Aaron Middleton. (Photo courtesy of Aaron Middleton.)

Brian and Carl Strong at summit of Red Hill Spur Trail, overlooking Devil's Gulch, Wenatchee National Forest, September 2011.

Brian's bike at Hell's Gate State Park, Lewiston, ID, overlooking the Snake River, September 2007. (Photo by Brian Johnson.)

Justin Moss on the rim of the Grande Ronde Canyon at Fields Spring State Park, Anatone, WA, May 2006.

Bob Dice at the Asotin Creek Trailhead, 15 miles WSW of Asotin, WA, April 2009.

Brian at the Asotin Creek Trail corral, approx. 5.4 miles from the trailhead, June 2010.

Three scenes from the B-23 wreckage at Loon Lake, Payette National Forest, Idaho, June 2009. From the top: Brian at the scene of the crash; remains of the B-23; the author, Brian and Jim Gentry. (Photo courtesy of Jim Gentry.)

Brian and the author during a break at a MAMBA trail building party, Moscow Mountain, Idaho, June 2006. (Photo by Kari Dickinson, used with permission.)

Front row of an impromptu rugby scrum, formed at the encouragement of Jerome Herro (center), Boundary Waters Canoe Area Wilderness, Minnesota, June 1989. (Photo courtesy of Jerome Herro.)

Brian Matthew Johnson: May 15, 1971 – August 3, 2014.

CPSIA information can be obtained
at www.ICGtesting.com
Printed in the USA
LVHW070223090121
675932LV00001B/2

9 781647 735869